grand-
mothers

grandmothers

ESSAYS BY
21ST-CENTURY GRANDMOTHERS

EDITED BY
HELEN ELLIOTT

TEXT PUBLISHING
MELBOURNE AUSTRALIA

textpublishing.com.au

The Text Publishing Company
Swann House
22 William Street,
Melbourne Victoria 3000,
Australia

First published in 2020 by The Text Publishing Company
Reprinted 2020

Book design by Imogen Stubbs
Cover design Chong W.H.
Typeset by J&M Typesetting

Printed and bound in Australia by Griffin Press, part of the Ovato group, an accredited ISO/NZS 14001:2004 Environmental Management System printer

ISBN: 9781922268600 (paperback)
ISBN: 9781925923223 (ebook)

A catalogue record for this book is available from the National Library of Australia

The dearest child is the child of your child.
EGYPTIAN PROVERB

Contents

Helen Elliott

Introduction

If nothing is going well, call your grandmother.
ITALIAN PROVERB

There are four of them. Olivia, Madeleine, Eloise and Isobel-Daisy. Sometimes I think they all belong to me. I sign my texts to the children and grandchildren The Doter.

Doting. Me, a woman who found the harnessing realities of early motherhood so crippling I couldn't wait for it to be over so I could get on with my own life. Now, this time of life, the final and perhaps loveliest part since my childhood, might be The Days of Doting.

Not all the women, the grandmothers, in the following pages, however, would be pleased to be called doters. Not at all! There is stringency in their words, as well as tenderness. Our commonality is in being a grandmother, and some of us here are more intentional grandmothers than others. Individuality flows through in grandmothering as much as it does through mothering. And in doting *now* there is, perhaps, an element of reparation for *then*.

When I was thirty, with a hard-won education behind me, my son was born. He was the first baby I had ever held. I had never understood what it was with women and babies. In fact, my mother came to stay for a while because she was 'worried about the baby'. And me. But for me it was love, love, love. And a terrifying responsibility. My mother went home and told everyone she was amazed. Two years later I had my daughter.

Grandmothering has always been a grand subject, but it has never been outed as such. There has been no strong narrative about grandmothering; it is still closeted. Too general to have interesting meaning, too often spoken about in a thoughtless, patronising tone. In a world where currency is all, 'like a granny' describes someone who is not current. 'Nanna nap' is insulting, as you will see in these essays. The grandmother narrative is circumscribed, lazily connected to scented soap, lace, lavender, babysitting, caregiving—a latter-day invisibility. Grandmother still suggests a woman whose days of significance in the actual, rushing world are past.

Yet. Yet. French president Emmanuel Macron says that his grandmother, whom he called Manette, was the most important adult in his life. Margaret Atwood is winning prizes, Hillary Clinton and Elizabeth Warren are not off-stage. In fiction, Lady Olenna, played by the obviously immortal Diana Rigg in *Game of Thrones*, is an archetype with nuance—a grandmother with knowledge of poison equal to her knowledge of power. And there is always Nancy Pelosi. Is it possible that she, too, might be immortal? I dare hope. Grandmothers can be the thing that surveys show is what a high number of young people aim to be, Influencers.

The essays in this book arrive from a reconfigured world. Grandmothers used to be the aged mother a loving child looked after. Now things have reversed, and more often than not the grandmother is essential to the smooth working of a busy family. The women here see themselves as current. Some are central in a family in an emotional sense and often in a financial sense. If the grandmother could not care for grand-children, the parent might not be able to work.

Women of my generation—I am speaking narrowly, specifically of certain strata of white women here—can be grateful to the feminist revolution of the sixties and seventies. Many more of us can also be grateful to the continuing technological revolution, where speed and connection have physical meaning in our daily lives. Connectivity is eloquent and satisfying and these essays are a testament to that. In the last thirty years, the world sped up more than it did in the previous three hundred. And the tech-savvy tell us that this is just the beginning of the change. Will we live long enough to see our grandchildren with phones implanted in their hands? Or chips in their temples for instant access to the internet? Some of us will.

We, too, are transforming, but in different ways. We are, perhaps, responding to the world, rather than creating it. A grandmother has transformed into something else, a grand mother. A great mother. We can't all be adept at practical poison, like Lady Olenna, but we have knowledge, experience, and, thanks to high tech, the world is paying attention in a new way. Grandmothers have a fresh visibility and are prepared to use it. There is grandmother Fonda, Jane, being arrested in New York as she draws attention to climate change. Climate change, unsurprisingly, is the urgent issue for most of the writers in this anthology.

Being a mother took some figuring out and so does being a grandmother. The grandmothers in the following pages often speak about the significance of their own grandmothers. We might not have paid attention back then. Children don't. Grandma was just grandma, by whatever name. Now our often surprising and surprised landing at this point in our lives allows the long view and we see that our grandmothers were, like us, more than just old women—some, astonishingly, were younger than we are now—from whom we might have inherited manners, hair, cancer, kindness, attention, generosity, impatience, vanity. That list is endless, intriguing and expands daily. The inheritance from a grandmother is worth an entire essay itself.

Women, constrained by culture and society, will turn to two things. Walking and gardening. All that walking in Jane Austen and the Brontës was not accidental. My love of gardening and of flowers came from my only grandmother, my mother's mother. She came to live with us when I was ten and died when I was fifteen. She was sick, she trembled, she was slow and I was a snippy girl, impatient as the wind. We didn't get on. Perhaps we loved one another? There is always something about blood connection. She knew about hard work and she knew about flowers.

In my thirties, I discovered why gardening is so attractive to women. Not just the women I knew from books but women I was meeting. Gardening is about cherishing and, critically for me, gardening meant I didn't have to play endless boring games with (cherished) toddlers. Instead we could garden together. My resentment at finding myself a mother was dug into the garden, buried as we watered and tended beautiful things that would flourish in the sunshine. It still astonishes me how simple it is to make children happy.

But the world has moved on and, close to the city where my children and their families live, gardens are seen as luxury. There are great public gardens that are still valued in Australia, but as much as I love these gifts from public planners of the past with a vision of a future, as much as I enjoy being in them, they don't offer the intimate pleasure of a private garden. A private garden can be a work of art and, like all good art, requires labour and concentration.

Our tranquil house, built on the lower slope of a mountain, rests in an acre of garden. We bought the house, the garden, with the grandchildren in mind. Children need gardens where they can be a bit wild and perhaps get up to mischief. The original owner of this house was a map collector and along the entire length of the hall are his map drawers. They are now filled not with maps, or anything important, but with the everyday mess of life. It is all a pleasure and mystery to my granddaughters. They've laid claim to these drawers as much as they've laid claim to the garden.

The boundary to the garden is a deep creek that rushes down the mountain, threatening to change course and break the banks if we don't clear it out over summer. The girls love to climb down onto the boulders and hurl whatever they can find up to the top. Last summer I was hit in the eye by something hurled. 'Fuck!' I yelled, clutching my head. Silence hung in the clear air.

Then: 'Grandma. You. Swore.'

This garden will stay with these children forever, regardless of the future. Like Grandma Fonda, like so many of the women in this book, I mourn the passing of the old natural world, alarmed at the prospect of the new world that climate change has made. If my granddaughters have a memory of a real garden, they might do something practical to help restore the natural world and the creatures in it as they create their own lives.

They ask me: what's that scent? Boronia? Daphne? They remember that hellebore is another name for Christmas rose. They love picking and arranging flowers and they raid the lemon trees with too much vigour, heady with the scent. From me they learned about the Greek myths and now they talk about the gods in that Arcadian world as if they were strolling on the footpath with us. 'Helen was the most beautiful woman in the world, Grandma. Did you know that?'

Human nature doesn't change, but the external world

does, sometimes enough to terrify us. This generation of grandmothers has assets that previous generations had to do without. We will be useful to social planners and policy-makers, and to historians, because they can track the changes through us. We were the immensely privileged generation who changed the idea of being a mother because, unlike our grandmothers, we had the possibility of an education.

Education is a theme in many of these essays, because it transforms everything. Not just us, but our children and grandchildren. Many of us saw the frustrations of the narrow path our post-war mothers had no choice in taking, because men were in financial control. Those women's lives were dedicated to the lives of their husbands and their families, but it turned out that a washing machine and vacuum cleaner didn't help with the amorphous restlessness defined by Betty Freidan. My generation didn't want our mother's life; we could not begin to imagine our grandmother's life. We are the generation who, instead of surrendering to motherhood and wifehood, heeded the poet Mary Oliver's narcissistic but revolutionary question in her poem 'The Summer Day': 'Tell me, what is it you plan to do / with your one wild and precious life?'

The twenty-two essays and stories in this book are the result of hard work and hard thought. They are written with emotional honesty and intellectual generosity by women from diverse backgrounds, all connected by the single, transitioning word *grandmother*. All these grandmothers are still in the process of forging their own lives. I don't like to use the word *wisdom*, because getting older doesn't mean you get any wiser, but, if you are lucky, by the time you are called grandmother you find an ability to see beyond your self and perhaps have some self-perception. On the evidence of these essays, you certainly have a wider understanding of how that glorious activity of the heart, *love*, can flourish. The surprise of grand-mothering is that the love works as an exhange; *beloved* I call them. *Beloved* they call me.

Helen Garner

Another Chance

One day in 1999, when I was rattling along with my broken heart on a Sydney suburban train, re-reading Thackeray's novel *Vanity Fair* for the comfort of its racy sentimentality and sly laughter, I turned a page and saw this sentence: 'A woman, until she is a grandmother, does not often really know what to be a mother is.'

I got out my notebook and copied it down. I didn't know why. I was not a grandmother. I didn't know whether or when I could hope to become one. I would have killed for my daughter—it was through her that I'd learnt what love is—but I'd never thought I was much chop as a mother: selfish, revved up, distracted by sex and romance, working like a maniac. Twenty years later, though, I understand that deep in the wreckage of my last marriage, in a corner of it still invisible to me, Thackeray's insight had lit a tiny spark. The gods were about to offer me another chance.

●

'We're having a baby,' wrote my daughter in Melbourne. 'You can come home now.'

●

The child slid into the world with ease. Her eyes were closed, her mouth curved in an expression of optimistic calm. I crouched against the wall of the birth suite, thunderstruck.

●

I must have driven them crazy. I was always rushing across town from my big empty house, bustling in and out, bringing things they didn't need, giving advice, staying too long. I battled to discipline myself, to ration my visits, to hide my jealousy of every other blow-in who held her. What I wanted was to be of use, but I didn't know how to conduct myself. The baby's parents were patient with me. I hope I washed up as often as I think I did.

●

Yet the baby as she grew seemed to like me. She smiled when she heard my voice. Her existence, my acquaintance with her, began to change my relationship with the world. How driven and ridiculous my former life now appeared to me! When I was near her I lost all sense of haste. Around her hummed a benign aura, a timeless atmosphere in which my harried spirit relaxed and expanded.

Soon after she got here I was offered a weekly newspaper column. Write anything you like! I would need to collect material. I got out a manila folder and labelled it 'Ideas'. My first deadline approached. I opened the file and looked inside. The lofty, important topics upon which I had planned to expatiate had shrivelled and died.

I cast my eyes around the room in a panic.

And there she lay behind me, on her little lamb's wool rug: my saviour.

•

They bought a house in the inner west. They said it would take my son-in-law six months to make a proper kitchen and bathroom. They asked if the three of them could come and live at my place for the duration. They wanted to *live* with me? I held my breath in case they changed their minds.

In my big bare kitchen certain patterns established themselves. She liked to crawl under a wooden chair and wedge herself there in a cage of legs and struts, peeping out like a cheerful bus driver. Or she sat on her father's lap in front of the TV, brightly erect against his chest, with her right thumb in her mouth and her left arm thrust out in a rigid line from shoulder to forefinger, pointing tirelessly at the screen where cartoon characters capered or David Attenborough murmured about silt on the River Nile.

Or she sat on the lino and gestured for me to sit behind her like a pillion passenger. She wrenched open a cupboard door, pulled out packets of pasta and slung them over her shoulder at me, one by one, without a glance. I caught with my right hand, and with my left slipped each packet back into the cupboard to replenish her supply. Now and then she turned and placed a packet precisely into my hand, as if we were working together in a shop.

Or she hauled the clean tea towels out of their drawer and spread them on the floor. I folded and stacked them. She scrunched them up and stuffed them back into the drawer, then began again her precise, rhythmic removals.

We never tired of these strange games she devised, so absorbing and repetitive, with their mysterious, pre-verbal meaning, demanding powerful concentration, seamless co-operation and complete silence.

When she got big enough, I would strap her into the seat on the back of my bike, early in the morning so her parents could catch up on sleep, and we'd pedal away along the bike track, across Royal Park and past the zoo as the sun came up. One morning she was silent behind me for so long that I put my foot on the ground and turned to check. Her helmet had slid right forward and down her nose, completely covering her eyes. Twin worms of creamy snot had reached her top lip. She was just poking her tongue out to staunch the flow. She couldn't see a thing. She had nothing to say and no language to say it in. She trusted me. She was content.

Her gift to me, apart from the joy of her presence, was

the fact that the world around her sprang into sharp focus. Boredom ceased to exist. Everything I looked at throbbed with meaning. My attention was drawn to and gratified by trivial matters I would once have trudged straight past: rain pattering on a stretched umbrella, a broken bead bangle, a high rose window shining in a dark church, a foul-mouthed junkie on a train, mud-caked boys slogging after a slimy football. Never before had I got such pleasure from writing, or from working to such a tight and inflexible word count. I turned in a column every week about a suburban world whose unexpected beauty refreshed my soul. The smaller the subject, the more intensely it rewarded me. At a family party, a distant in-law said she'd been reading me in the paper. I flinched. She hit me with a comment that I took at first for a backhander, then recognised as the best compliment I'd ever received—an articulation, in fact, of an unconscious artistic credo.

'A little bit of nothing,' she said, 'and suddenly, there's a story.'

*

I know how tedious grandparents can be, with our mushy boasting and besotted smiles, so I tried to keep the child *as subject* to a minimum—as if it were indecent to reveal such primal, unreasoning, undeserved happiness before strangers. But sometimes I couldn't help myself; every time I let my guard down I would sense again my membership of an obscure and incredulous sisterhood. One night, in the lobby of the concert hall, a woman I'd never met, but whose husband, so I'd heard, had left her for someone younger, came up to me and said in a very soft voice, 'Thank you for your column. I'm a grandmother too, now. I didn't know there was another love.'

•

It took nearly two years for them to make their house right. We never had a quarrel. But on the day they drove away, the little girl wouldn't kiss me goodbye. From her point of view, I was leaving her. She wouldn't look at me or speak to me for a week.

A year or so later, their next-door neighbour stuck her head over their fence and said she was putting her house on the market. It was the same as their house, except that it had the one thing my son-in-law craved: a shed.

The day I got possession, I called them to say I had the key and was on my way. By the time I got there, twenty minutes later, my son-in-law was out in the yard with his chainsaw, slicing a hole in the side fence. I stood outside my new back door and watched. The saw screamed. The grey timber parted and fell. And through the gap came parading a small colourful figure, arrayed in trailing draperies, tap shoes, and an enormous broad-brimmed hat with nodding ostrich feathers. She clicked and clacked across the brick paving to the bottom step of my verandah. 'This,' she said, 'is the happiest day of my life.'

•

Then, somehow, everything speeded up. Soon there came a boy, who looked like an owl, then another, who was chunkier, more like a boxer. The world stretched again and exploded into new configurations. The owlish one loved to dress in tutus, horror masks and huge wigs. The boxer stumped about in an ankle-length overcoat with big brown lapels.

The girl learned the pleasures of being older and bossier. She went to school. From our station platform, on my way to the city, I could see the window of her upstairs classroom, where between jobs I sometimes helped with reading practice, jammed into a narrow couch beside some earnestly stumbling little boy. I longed to lift the slow readers into my lap, to ease their struggles, but it was not permitted, and anyway they had their own nannas at home, so my finger moved along the lines and we laboured away together, shoulder to shoulder, murmuring and pausing and trying again. Then the teacher would clap, and get out his guitar and play a song he'd written especially for his class: 'We are the children of Prep 1A, Prep 1A, Prep 1A…' Proudly they sang, beaming up at him from the floor.

·

At home we got a red heeler, two cats, and four chickens. If you didn't count the livestock, we had gender equality, not that anyone cared. Foxes killed some of the chickens and we bought new ones from the feed shop near the racecourse. We knocked down the whole fence and the yard was wide. We put in rainwater tanks. We pulled down the termite-ridden shed and built a better one. We planted fruit trees and grew big crops of broad beans and tomatoes.

It became clear to us that this was a natural way for a family to live. Adults were not outnumbered by kids. Childcare could bounce between us, according to circumstance. I worked freelance and could be flexible. My daughter could go back to university and become a high-school teacher. Her husband could work at night in his bands, and paint in his shed by day, and hang out washing, and prune his trees, and build chook pens, and cook up a storm. No one was ever bored or lonely. There was always something happening. I might have been a flop at marriage, and scrappy as a mother, but as a grandmother I didn't need to fight for a place to stand. I knew my place. I could *serve*. I was useful, and free, and fed, and endlessly entertained.

•

I had four sisters and one brother, and my only child was a daughter. I'd known a lot of men, but I had never raised a boy. I didn't know how different they were, the particular tone of their concentration, their delicacy, the needs they had and the kinds of games that answered to those needs.

The owl-boy, for example, instituted a cowboy empire that he invited me into a hundred times. Its rules and customs were unchanging, its boundaries firmly enforced. I learned my part and performed it faithfully on demand, never suggesting fresh developments or asking literal-minded questions. It gratified both of us deeply, in ways we never thought to articulate.

'Nanny,' he would say in a voice of yearning, 'do you know where they sell spurs?' The answer to this was always no. But one day, mooching through a hardware store in Geelong, I came across a shiny, clanking pair. I bought them and rushed home. 'Hey, hey! Guess what I got you!' He glanced at them with an expression of aggrieved incredulity, and walked out into the backyard. We never played that game again.

The game called Hotels lasted juicily, with parts for all three of them and me, for a good year, until one day the girl got impatient and set up the ironing-board reception desk and old red telephone too fast, without observing the niceties of preparation. The owl-boy burst into wild sobs of rage and sorrow, and dashed out of the room. That one, too, he would never play again. I still miss it: the room service orders laboriously taken down by phone, the checking out, the 'arguments' over the fairness of bills…we would go on for hours, running up and down 'stairs', serving each other, 'losing our tempers', being a posh lady or a rude guest or an overworked supervisor. Privately I link it with the time my father made a fuss over a restaurant bill; when it was over and he had won, he sat back happily and said, 'I've never *seen* such a deflated manager!'

The boxer is an easygoing guy. His needs are simple. He enjoys a thrash on the ukes and then a game of Snap. I put on a Frank Sinatra CD and we sit there slapping down the cards, shouting and shuffling, and singing along: 'Moon shining down/ on some little town…' In their own house these kids have been authoritatively exposed since early childhood to the full power of

'Midnight Special' and 'Soul Train'. They are experts on James Brown. I fill in the gaps with 'Tubby the Tuba', or sneak in a track from *Die Schöne Müllerin*.

•

They bring their class photos home and I examine the faces one by one, asking for names and character sketches. The girl is brilliant at this but the boys are hopeless. They have only one word to describe a girl classmate. Me: '*She* looks nice. What's she like?' Grandson: 'Annoying.' 'And this one here— what a clever face. What sort of person is she?' 'Annoying.' 'How about this tiny one with the grin?' 'An*noy*ing.'

•

It's a grandmother's prerogative to run a tight ship. I remember my father's stepmother, when I went to stay with them, putting a strip of old towel under my bed to stand the potty on, 'lest you soil the carpet'. At my place, boys may not tilt their chairs. One evening, when they were being oafish at the table, I hustled them out onto the back verandah, slammed and locked the door, and shouted, 'You can stay out there *all night*.' I disposed myself on the couch and self-righteously leafed through a magazine. Night was falling. On the other side of the wall the boxer snivelled and the owl-boy whispered at great length. After a while they fell silent. I went on pretending to read. It was a chilly evening and I was starting to wonder how I could back down before their parents got home. I opened the door. There they sat on the step in the dark, like two foundlings. They looked up at me. I said stiffly, 'You can come in now.' They followed me in, and took their seats at the table before their plates of congealed food. They pulled in their chairs and wielded their cutlery with decorum. 'Where were you planning to sleep?' I asked. '*He* wanted to sleep with the dog,' replied the owl-boy, 'so we'd be warm. But I said there'd be fleas.' 'And,' said the boxer, on whose cheeks the tears had left long, dirty streaks, '*he* said we'd have to make a little nest. Under a bush.' That was when we all started to laugh.

•

When it's my turn I drive them to footy training and some-times to their matches. I knew I needed cataract surgery when I ceased to be able to pick them out of the pack on the other side of the ground. Not by their numbers. I don't need numbers. I know them by the shape of their skulls and the set of their shoulders, the way their hair swings or sticks up, the length of their strides.

•

'Will you watch something on TV with me?' says the boxer after school.

'Why do you want me to watch with you?'

'Because,' he says without missing a beat, 'you make witty comments and smart cracks.'

I forget whether it was Rochefoucauld or Richelieu who said, '*Tu me flattes; mais continue.*'

•

Meanwhile the girl sings, swots, cooks, surfs, plays AFL: the fearless filth of her, the bouncing ponytail! The black armband! The tackles, the falls! The ambulance that comes for her teammate who's knocked out cold! Is this the same child who at six came home from her first flamenco lesson? Who, when her mother and I asked how it had gone, did not speak but straightened her spine, lowered her brow, and flung up one arm in a posture of such dignified command that our smiles slid off our faces?

When she needed a teenage bedroom we knocked the two houses into one and she moved across into my spare room. The owl-boy surveyed the new arrangement and said, 'I've always wanted to live in a mansion.'

And now she's gone to Europe. She worked four part-time jobs, got on a plane with her friends and flew away. How will we live without her singing round the house? I keep her bedroom door closed. I don't want to see the bedraggled grey velvet shark lying on the stripped bed, the line of shoes, the chair facing the bare desktop, the guitar. The day after she left, her mother and I came home from our respective work-places and met by chance in their kitchen. We stopped and stared. Each of us had gone out that morning without a word and had her hair cut. We hardly knew whether we were living in a fairytale or a myth.

'How are *you* without her?' she said.

'Oh, it's empty. And quiet.'

We've never been the sort of mother and daughter who hug a lot. We stood there looking out the window at the winter yard.

'Maybe I should send over one of the boys,' she said. 'As a replacement.'

We bowed over her kitchen bench on our elbows, in a helpless convulsion.

Ali Cobby Eckermann

Grandmothers' Law Should Never Be Broken

First Time (I Met My Grandmother)

Sit down in the dirt and brush away the flies
Sit down in the dirt and avoid the many eyes

I never done no wrong to you, so why you look at me?
But if you gotta check me out, well go ahead—feel free!

I feel that magic thing you do, you crawl beneath my skin
To read the story of my Soul, to find out where I been

And now yous' mob you make me wait, so I just sit and sit
English words seem useless, I know Language just a bit

I sit quiet way, not lonely, 'cos this country sings loud Songs
I never been out here before, but I feel like I belong

It's three days now, the mob comes back, big smiles
are on their faces
'This your Grandmother's Country here, this is
your homeland place'

'We got a shock when we seen you, you got your Nana's face
We was real sad when she went missing in that cold
Port Pirie place'

I understand the feelings now, tears push behind my eyes
I'll sit on this soil anytime, and brush away the flies

I'll dance with mob on this red Land, *munda wiru* place
I'll dance away them half caste lies 'cos I got my Nana's face!

From *little bit long time*, 2009

Grandmothers' Law Should Never Be Broken

Let no-one say the past is dead.
The past is all about us and within.

From 'The Past', *The Dawn Is at Hand*, 1964
Oodgeroo Noonuccal, 1920–1993

•

In the night someone strung a line of crow carcasses across the fence outside her house. She discovers them as she leaves the house for work. Her breath catches in her chest and she cannot breathe. Jesus! she mutters, half in anger and half in a plea to the heavens. Who would do such a thing? Unable to move, her entire body is frozen with shock. She dares not look at the dull eyes on their avian faces, the heads hanging as if dangling on broken necks. Her hands rise, as if by free will to cover her mouth, to stifle the scream she feels growing inside her chest. It is inaudible. She vomits a mouthful of dark bile into her palms. The darkness acts like a mirror and she stares at the reflection she holds in her cupped hands. It is her grandmother's face transforming to crow.

In the backyard of the tenement house the young woman's actions are frantic. Her hands are filthy now, covered with dirt from the large hole she has dug in the ground. She gathers twigs from under the hedge to add to a small fire she has lit next to the hole. She paces between as if undecided. She kneels to scoop more dirt into the grave, bends to gather more kindling for the fire. Squatting on her haunches, she rolls her head back to stare at the sky. It is cloudless, as empty as her shaking heart. Her head flops forward and she sobs into her hands. Through her tears she senses the arrival of her, and quickly wipes her tears in a muddy streak across her face. A willie wagtail hops across the dry lawn to her side. They crouch together, staring in silence into the fire.

•

Birds. The adventure of feeling an association with birds was taught to me by my familial grandmother, whom I first met when I was thirty-four, in the red desert of central Australia, at the small community where she was living. Nana was a petite woman filled with warm laughter, with an engaging smile and a shock of white hair. I was the second of her Stolen-Generation grandchildren to return home. Now in her senior years, she was respectfully retired from work and always made time to sit and talk, telling story after story, as if making up for those lost years. In the late afternoon we sat outside her house in the shade of the water tank while she *sang* the birds, feeding them titbits as they arrived. I watched, fascinated, as some flew onto her lap, chirping to her as if joining her laughter. A few years later, Nana moved to Coober Pedy. She was a founding member of *Kupa Piti Kungka Tjuta*, a heroic group of senior Aboriginal women who in 1998 headlined a challenge against the Australian government to prevent a nuclear waste dump on their traditional land, and won their case in 2004.

The Stuart Highway cuts through the centre of Australia from Darwin in the north, through Alice Springs, to Port Augusta in the south. It is one of Australia's major highways and the opal-mining town of Coober Pedy rests on its rim. On warm sunny days I would sit on Nana's verandah in the company of her dogs, listening to her childhood stories of growing up in the bush before the saga of the nuclear testing by the British on our traditional lands at Maralinga. If the weather was too hot or too cold, we camped on mattresses in her dimly lit lounge room, peering at faded black-and-white photographs of people who had passed. She kept this stash of photographs hidden in a handbag in her bedroom and brought them out to teach me our family tree. There was always laughter and the sharing of food. I loved every opportunity to care for her; it was a blessing prompted by cultural exchange. As Nana grew more frail, she moved into the local aged-care facility where most of the *Kupa Piti Kungkas Tjuta* spent their final years. Through the kinship system, I was proud to regard most of these cultural law women as my grandmothers. Those years with Nana before she died were among my happiest.

Many Aboriginal people know the willie wagtail bird as the messenger bird. This small black-and-white-feathered fantail is often known to bring news when loved ones have died. I saw it once relentlessly flying against a windowpane to gain attention, minutes before the phone call arrived, confirming a family member had died. I used to chase them away. My grandmother and her cousin-sisters would sing to them, inviting them to join us, laughing at my nervousness. I learned that these birds also bring good news, and are guardians. In Yankunytjatjara culture, all bird names are their call. The willie wagtail is *tjintar-tjintar.* The crow is *kaanka.* Both birds have become essential to my holistic health.

It is common sense that if one stays in one location for a long amount of time, one will learn to know that place in a more intimate way. My traditional family has lived on our traditional lands for over eighty thousand years. Anthropological science has proved that Aboriginal culture is the longest living continuous culture on this planet. A job opportunity in my early forties provided me with the chance to be closer to my traditional Anangu family and live with them in the desert. Within their 'university' of ancient knowledge I was their 'mature-age student', who had a voracious appetite to learn. Guidance from a select group of senior women and men was grounded and sage; I listened to their every word. As they retired and moved into aged care, I returned to the south. At forty-five, I bought the old General Store in Koolunga, just south of Port Pirie in South Australia, establishing Australia's first Aboriginal Writers Retreat. I replayed—over and over in my heart and mind—the ethics and memories of those poignant years learning from Nana and the other Elders. The vividness of recent memory began to override unpleasant memories of the racism I had endured during my youth as an adopted child. With my new knowledge, I could enjoy resting in bed, listening for the first bird call of the day. Often, I would gain energy and momentum from the bird calls that were most familiar to me. The knowledge of birds has become an ongoing ritual of focus for me. Familiar bird calls act as spiritual affirmations to my heart and reassurances that those I love are nearby: I am loved by nature, and I am not alone.

I remember too, in the late 1960s, when lines of wedge-tailed eagle carcasses were strung along roadside fences in the mid-north of South Australia where I lived. It was a ruthless practice adopted by sheep farmers. The sight of it horrified me as a girl. I used to stare from the rear passenger window of my parents' car as we drove past. Sometimes I dared not look at their regal faces and closed my eyes quickly. My adopted father was a gentle man and certainly did not condone cruelty. One of my male adopted cousins was the main offender in our family when it came to these killings; he would ridicule me until I fell silent, insisting that the birds were vermin, shot to protect the newborn lambs in the paddocks. It took me years to forgive him.

I also remember the large mosaic of Jesus above the altar in the local church where we worshipped every Sunday as a family, how Jesus stood in a meek stance of reclamation, displaying the wounds on his hands and bare feet. I remember knowing in my heart that Jesus would not accede to the eagles being killed, their wings stretched open and wired onto the strands of barbed-wire fencing in a feathered crucifixion.

Before school, I spent a lot of time with Dad on the farm; I was known as *his little shadow*. I can recall a faint memory from 1972 of sitting at the kitchen table for lunch when the radio broadcast a new National Parks and Wildlife Act that gave protection to these majestic eagles. In Yankunytjatjara language, the wedged-tail eagle is *walawaru*. I always feel safer when I see *walawaru* soaring the skies. I see them often and know they watch over me.

•

Since the death of Nana, and all the many other caring, wise, senior women who welcomed me back into my family, including my mother and her sisters, I have travelled extensively across Australia and overseas. Everywhere, my eyes are trained to watch for birds. Using cultural knowledge, Nana taught me how to see, how to watch. In Australia, wherever I travel, both *tjintar-tjintar* and *kaanka* are always close by. *Tjintar-tjintar* is the message bird, the dancer who delivers both good and sad news. No longer fearful, I feel reassured by his presence. *Kaanka* has become my most defining bird. I believe she is my Nana, still guiding me. When I hear her call, I am immediately inclined to regard my actions and words with kindness, as she instructed. Often, she greets me in the early morning as I leave for exercise or work. Most evenings, when the sun is closest to the horizon, she sits outside my house talking loudly, reminding me of the importance of self-evaluation and responsibility. *Kaanka* reminds me to remember Nana's teachings, and to stay humble as I journey on my path.

It has been my privilege to learn snippets from cultures outside my own. In 2018, I travelled to Colombia in South America, to attend and present at the 28th International Poetry Festival of Medellín, which celebrates both shamanism and poetry. During the opening ceremony, the shamans welcomed us. This seven-day event was an incredible experience for me. During my time in Medellín, I met with three South American women poets: Negma Coy (Maya Nation) from Guatemala, Alba Eiraji Duarte Portillo (Guarini) from Paraguay, and Rayen Kvych (Mapuche) from Chile. Through an interpreter, we spent time talking about the Stolen Generations and the sadness I carry inside me. This ongoing chapter of Australian history shocked and saddened these cultured women. They explained to me that Grandmothers' Law should never be broken; it is a cultural law that should remain intact. My new friends reminded me of the importance of my role as grandmother: to mentor a positive and encouraging presence; to affirm a loving companionship; and to foster a long view of family connection, as all children crave a sense of belonging.

These women reminded me that Grandmothers' Law is an ancient law, bound through all indigenous cultures. They were appalled that the sanctity of Grandmothers' Law for Aboriginal Australians has, for generations, been broken by ongoing government policies of child removal. I remember them saying in dismay, 'Even war doesn't do that!' These three generous women told me about the Grandmother Ceremony they honour in each of their villages, and assured me that they would pray for the grandmothers who have suffered the traumatic legacy of the Stolen Generations. And, through the interpreter, we prayed together for the rich and sacred blessing of grandmothers to continue in all our families.

My first grandchild was through kinship, as was her mother. There was always an invitation to join in caring for her. She is now seventeen. In my experience, it is a different and often difficult role as a Stolen Generations grandmother. Some parents of adopted children shift their duty, allowing and inviting space for the birth parent(s) when they arrive. I see this gesture as both accepting and empathetic; the rights and wellbeing of the child are of primary importance. Some adoptive parents cling tightly to the child, even when the child is an adult in the process of working out their identity, at a time when they may be emotional about the past. When conflict arises, human nature seeks what it has known. I have witnessed emotional bribery, when relinquishment has been neither forgiven nor forgotten, as if there is a permanent stain of character on the birth mother. Healthy relationships grow slowly, even those of blood. Some adoptive parents sabotage the reunion.

For me, there has been no easy path around the relinquishment of my son and the issue of adoption. In my experience, the rights of the birth mother have been relegated to second place. If the adopted parents are reluctant to co-share the grandparent role, it feels so unkind if they also persuade the adopted child to snub the birth parent(s). As an Aboriginal grandmother, I feel I am constantly punished for a decision I was forced to make when I was a teenager. It has become a guilt returned to me over and over, a guilt from which I will never be released. I feel I have become the wedged-tail eagle carcass tied to the fence, crucified by the moral code that could not prevent the removal of myself as a baby from my mother. This is what intergenerational separation and trauma feel like on a daily basis. I do not get the opportunity to state my case: there has been no counsel for reconnection as yet.

In Australia there is a self-driven organisation called Grandmothers Against Removal, a grassroots organisation started in 2014 by First Nations community members directly affected by forced child removals. GMAR is a community group that advocates against the forced removal of First Nations children from their immediate and extended families and works to prevent further Stolen Generations. GMAR supports families in navigating the child protection system and lobbies government and child-protection agencies for self-determination and improved outcomes for First Nations children. This organisation needs all the support it can get.

After a period of threatened absence, I cherish every moment spent with my two young grandsons, however intermittent this is. At first, my time with my grandchildren required personal private time for my healing, as I had rarely held a baby since losing my own. My time with my grandsons taught me exactly what I had lost through the relinquishment of their father. This after-effect hit me so unexpectedly; I had not foreseen those brutal tears. It remains important to me that my young grandsons know my *essence*. It became obvious that we all respond best to time spent together out bush. I can teach them about the wind and birds, and fire. This is where I feel happiest and more relaxed. I want them to know me in my wholeness, the way I knew the wholeness of my grandmother.

I miss holding my Nana's hand so much. I know she continues to hold mine.

•

Alone, she pretends happiness. She hums softly to herself as she washes her face and body, early risen and indebted to the genesis of each day as she was taught, smiling ever so slightly at the sepia photograph of her grandmother that rests permanently on the polished rosewood ledge above the white porcelain sink.

Unhurriedly, she gets dressed into the uniform of routine and manual labour that she wears to work each morning. A greying sky hangs heavy over the grey cobblestone road as she exits the bluestone house, pausing only to slip her hand into her blue-grey blouse, tucking the latchkey inside her bra. She nods to the black crow perched on the electricity pole above her. Kaanka. *Its call is long and loud, repeated as if in greeting. Her footsteps are silent as she walks to catch the train to the city. The crow flits from pole to pole above her.* Tjintar-tjintar *flits close by.*

Jane Caro

Pass It On

'Can I give you a kiss goodbye?'

I always ask my three-year-old grandson for permission before I give him a hug or a kiss. We are very big on consent in our family and believe in teaching respect for another's bodily autonomy early, but sometimes (often) it has its downside.

'No, you can't.'

I respect his choice—I have to, that's the point of asking— but I don't give up entirely.

'Can I shake your hand instead, then?'

He looks up at me sweetly and replies with exactly the right note of kindly condescension and regret.

'No, sorry, you can't. I am just too busy.'

Once again, I must content myself with a wave and blowing a kiss. His little sister, not yet verbal, loves to give big, open-mouthed, sloppy kisses and, despite her snotty nose, I'm happy with that.

I love being a grandmother. I love it in a way that surprises me. When my daughter first announced she was pregnant—with my perennially time-poor grandson, as it turned out—I was pleased, of course, but I also felt an unexpected clutch of anxiety. Ever since my daughters moved out of home, I have revelled in my child-free existence. I love the freedom to work, loll about, watch what I want, eat what I want, when I want (with only minor objections from my husband). I love that when I tidy up, it stays tidy and I love the peace and quiet. I love the freedom to travel, to come and go as I please. I loved it so much that when our two cats died within months of one another, I had zero desire to replace them. That's why I worried—guiltily—what the return of little children into my life would do to my blissful and professionally satisfying existence.

And, of course, my two grandchildren have blown up my life. Not as much as they have blown up my daughter's, but enough to have taken most of my down time. What is surprising is that I don't mind. I look forward to seeing Alfie and Esther with the anticipation of a teenage girl with a crush, and I like who I am with them.

I am much more patient with my grandchildren than I was with my own daughters. I have just enough detachment—and more than enough energy, unlike their sleep-deprived mother—to observe their temper tantrums (they are real, human children, after all) without feeling either responsible or disturbed. My daughter tells me I am the master of distraction—I suppose it's the decades of experience as a mother kicking in. It is always nice to discover old skills that have lain rusty for years and find you can still use them with skill and tact. I rarely lose my temper with my grandchildren. I do not mind mess, sticky fingers, the aforementioned snotty noses, spills or marks on furniture. I am not good at playing games or rumbling (I never was)—that is my husband's terrain—but I am great for reading stories, telling stories, drawing pictures, singing songs, going for walks, sploshing in puddles, rambling round the garden, watering plants (I don't even make too much fuss when I get hosed) and taking their conversation and observations seriously. I pay my grandson and my granddaughter serious attention. I hope I always will.

When I was in the grip of the small flare-up of anxiety that greeted my daughter's announcement of impending birth, I made a silent promise to myself: I would be as supportive of my daughter and her mothering as I possibly could be. I would not criticise—and I don't. (This is not hard because I generally agree with her parenting style.) I would help her out whenever she asked—if I possibly could. I would never let her see that I was putting time in reluctantly, even if I was. I remember with pain how bad I felt every time I asked my own mother for help—help I desperately needed. My mother had four children and by the time her grandchildren came around I think she had well and truly had enough. She loved her children's children, but she was protective of her hard-won freedom. When my sisters and I were young mothers, it was my mother's feminism that made her so reluctant to give up the space she had finally created for herself. It is my feminism that makes me so determined to help my own daughter as much as possible and never, ever make her feel guilty for asking. I remember how annihilating it was to drown beneath the demands of a toddler who wouldn't sleep during the day, a baby who wouldn't sleep at night and a husband whose job took him away twenty-six weeks a year. I do not want her to feel that way.

Perhaps it was those bad memories—my younger daughter's first year of life was one of the worst years of mine, mostly due to chronic sleep-deprivation—that triggered the frisson of anxiety when I first heard I was to be a grandmother. I was afraid that I might have to go down that dark rabbit hole a second time, but it has not turned out that way.

I underestimated just how much I would love these small but vigorous and insistent voyagers into the future—a future that I will never see, a future I now worry about even more. What will climate change do to their prospects? But that is an issue for a different essay. Just as I felt about my own children, I recognise that these grandchildren are my only chance for immortality or, at least, life after death—they will remember us. Their arrival has made me think about my own grandmothers, both of whom have been dead for decades. I only really knew my maternal grandmother and I loved her very much. She and my maternal grandfather followed their daughters (my mother and my aunt) when they migrated to Australia in the early 1960s. My paternal grandparents remained in London. I was five almost six when we migrated to Australia. I was ten nearly eleven when we travelled back to the UK in 1968. The day after we arrived was the last time I ever saw my London-based grandmother.

'My head! My head!'

My grandmother was in the front passenger seat of her car. My father was driving. They had decided that he should start getting used to driving on British roads again as we were intending to stay in the UK for months. It turned out to be a very wise decision.

My grandmother was screaming in terrible distress. It was an unearthly noise. I had never heard an adult make such a sound. We'd left my mother and three-year-old sister at the local laundrette with a promise to pick them up in an hour or so. We had a lot of laundry. My family, including four children aged from three (the previously mentioned baby sister) to ten (me) had been travelling for weeks. My other sister, brother and I were all in the back seat. I could see my father was very upset. None of us made a sound.

We got home and my grandmother was still moaning and screaming. She was writhing in pain and clutching her head. My father told us to go into the lounge room.

'You're in charge, Jane. Don't come out, no matter what you hear!'

He closed the door firmly behind him. I felt scared but also proud to have such a responsibility. I heard my father dial the ambulance. I heard the siren as it arrived—it sounded different from Aussie ones. I heard my grandmother screaming…and screaming…and screaming. But we did not come out, not one of us, or open the door, or ask any of the questions we were desperate to ask.

My sixty-three-year-old grandmother (she chose to be called Gran, not Granny because it made her sound too old) had suffered an aneurism. She died a few weeks later, leaving my parents and grandfather grief-stricken. It remains the one and only time I saw my father cry. But apart from that one dramatic and horrible moment, I have no memory of my paternal grandmother. When I think of her now that I am aged sixty-two, only one year younger than she was when she died, it is with sadness for her and fear for me. I don't want to die before my grandchildren can fix some memories of me. I want to stay alive for at least another twenty years— for all sorts of reasons, of course, but not least because I want my grandchildren to remember me, the way I remember my maternal grandmother.

In the more formal era of my youth, we all referred to my mother's mother as Granny Booth. To her face, we called her Granny. It was in her honour that I knew, as soon as my daughter announced her pregnancy, that I wanted to be called Granny. Like my long-dead other grandmother, many of my friends felt that Granny sounded too old; they preferred the more common Australian honorific of Nan or Nanna. But there has never been a Nan or a Nanna in my archetypical northern-English family and I felt Granny was right—both to honour my heritage and my own half-Scottish, half-Welsh Granny Booth. As it stands, the discussion has proven moot.

My grandson calls me Gonky, which is as close as he can come to Granny. I love it and answer happily to it when it is screamed out across a crowd of bemused shoppers in the local mall. My husband is Gra Ga and he likes that fine too. Indeed, my grandson has recently taken a liking to calling everyone a bin-truck, as in Gonky bin-truck, and I am quite delighted by that too—a grandmother's love is blind.

I loved my Granny Booth. Of all my relatives in my extended family, she is the only one who never judged me. I was a bumptious and outspoken child, hungry for the limelight. I was not what a nice little girl was meant to be, especially in the 1960s, and my overeagerness resulted in some people taking pleasure in squelching me. No doubt I often deserved it, but Granny never squelched me, nor did she ever make me feel that she disapproved of me. I just felt loved by her even though she would no more have demonstrated overt affection or said the words 'I love you' than flown to the moon. People from working-class Manchester don't hold with being mushy. She showed her affection in small ways. I was a picky eater and she was a bounteous and talented baker. When I watch *The Great British Bake-Off* now (and I cannot get enough of it) I often think how my quiet, self-effacing Granny could easily have won the competition if only such things had been around in her day. I still make her melt-in-your-mouth short pastry every Christmas…but I digress.

Granny Booth took the trouble to notice the baked goods I did like—scones, Shrewsbury biscuits, lemon curd, shortbread, cheese-and-onion pie—and made sure she always had plenty on hand. Like my own mother, she never forced me to eat anything I did not like. She knew what each of her grand-children (she had six, my mother's four and my aunt's two) liked best and had them freshly baked and plated up ready to be devoured when we came to see her. She was brilliant at handicrafts—I still have some lace she made by means of the long-forgotten art of tatting—and made us beautiful stuffed toys and an exquisite collection of elegant clothes for my Barbie doll—a collection I am ashamed to say I turned my nose up at because they were not store-bought. How I wish I still had them now. My elder daughter inherited that talent, and as I watch her knit and crochet blankets, toys and clothing, I always think how proud her great-granny would have been.

My sister who was closest to me in age was one of those kids who caught constant bouts of tonsillitis. I was never sick. When relatives came to see Ann in her sickbed, they would bring her a present. I'll never forget the time Granny brought me a small present as well and said, 'It's not your fault you are not sick.' She thought of things like that.

She was also great fun and up for a laugh, despite her natural reserve. We played charades every Christmas—the kind where you are on a team, choose a word and then act out each syllable while the other teams try to guess what full word you have chosen. At one family celebration, I vividly remember her playing a naughty schoolgirl in my cous-in's ill-fitting school uniform. It may even have been at her husband's and her golden wedding anniversary party. She was utterly convincing and filled with glee. It made me wonder what kind of a schoolgirl she once was.

I was with her just before she died. I went home to my children only a few hours before she took her last breath. My aunt and my cousin were with her at the end, and she died—as so few of us are fortunate enough to do—in her own bed. She died quickly, taking to her bed only a day or two before the end. I knew—as we all did—that she was fatally ill, but she was ninety-two, and at that age cancer proceeds slowly, so when I decided to take my two-year-old daughter to visit her, I had done so to alleviate the sense of aimlessness that often assailed me when I had dropped my elder daughter at school and the hours until I picked her up yawned in front of me. As the mother of small children, I could not escape the feeling that no one knew or cared what I did with my day, and I did not like it. To fill the time, I drove down to the retirement village where my grandmother—a widow by this time—lived. I had no idea that she was within a day or two of dying.

As soon as I saw her, however, I knew. My aunt was with her and had obviously stayed the night, but that was not what gave the game away. My ladylike Granny was sitting on the couch with her skirt rucked up above her thighs, oblivious to her *déshabillé*. But that wasn't the main clue either. It was her eyes. I know this sounds absurd, but they had the same huge pupils and unfocused, faraway look my cat had a few days before it passed away at a grand old age. As soon as I saw her eyes, I knew.

She wasn't unhappy, however, and she was conscious enough of her surroundings to be pleased to see us, particularly her great-granddaughter Charlotte (who bore Granny's mother's first name). Charlotte was as bubbly and unselfconscious as toddlers always are with people they know and love, and my gentle grandmother had my daughter's confidence just as much as she had mine. Charlotte clambered up beside her to play a favourite game—one I had also loved as a small child. Granny and Charlotte used an ancient set of dominoes (I suspect the white squares were made from real ivory) to build houses and towers, which of course two-year-old Charlotte delighted in knocking down. When the charms of that game palled, Charlotte went out into Granny's garden. Her bungalow in the retirement village had a spectacular flower garden, established by my long-dead grandfather and lovingly maintained by his wife. It was a beautiful day and Charlotte happily picked flowers. That was another great virtue of my granny—it pleased her to see children pick and enjoy the flowers she grew.

Charlotte came inside and climbed up again beside Granny on her makeshift bed on the couch. Entirely spontaneously, and prattling away cheerfully, my little blonde daughter began to weave the flowers she had picked into my grandmother's grey hair. My grandmother could not have been more delighted. It is the last picture I have in my mind's eye of my much-loved grandmother, a little old lady who looked rather like a wizened five-year-old—she had lost so much weight to the cancer—resplendent with bright flowers woven into her hair.

●

I hope my last conscious day is exactly like hers. But that is not why I tell you this story. I tell you because the fact that my grandmother remains so vividly in my memory is something that has taken on more importance to me now. Grandchildren give you a foothold into the future, for sure, but they also ladder you back to the past. In a strange way, becoming a grandmother, like becoming a mother, leads you to recognise connections, characteristics and legacies of those figures from your own childhood. Your memory of the grandmothers who preceded you sharpens. And the importance of them intensifies; your memory of them keeps them alive, just as their memory of their own grandparents did and still does. Granny Booth often told me stories of her own mother (Granny Jones) and grandmother (Granny Grey), and of her parents-in-law (she didn't like them much).

I have a great deal of information about the women of my family thanks to that chain of grandmothers. It saddens me, and is also revealing, that I know so little about the men. They kept themselves to themselves in a way that women do not.

Until very recently, the memories from my grandmother were all the information I had about my antecedents. I found out a little about the Caro side via some census information, and I knew Gran Caro was a professional dancer who once performed in a show with Fred Astaire's equally famous sister Adele. All the Caros are nifty movers—it's because we are hyper-mobile, which, especially as you age, turns out not to be a good thing.

It is due to modern technology, however, that I discovered the lost secret of the unbroken chain of my maternal grandmothers. I had my DNA tested a couple of years ago. It came about as part of the SBS promotion of their program *DNA Nation*. They wanted a Fairfax columnist to have their DNA tested to promote the show and I was the lucky writer who got the gig. My father and I swabbed our cheeks—fathers and daughters have to be tested separately to isolate the mitochondrial DNA because mothers pass it on to their daughters, not to their sons. We know maternal grandmothers are particularly important for the health and survival of their grandchildren, much more so than grandmothers on the father's side. We also know that it is their DNA that is handed down through the maternal line, from mother to daughter from generation to generation. The chain of grandmothers is not just emotional or practical, it is biological too.

As everyone knows, all modern humans have the same great-great-great-etc-grandmother—an African woman who lived 200,000 years ago. Along the way, however, her mitochondrial DNA has mutated many times, creating all the various differences we can see in human beings and their racial and ethnic identities today. These mutations are called haplotypes and are what identify your ancestry when you have your DNA tested. People who look like me—white Europeans—are usually haplotype H, a mutation that occurred about 30,000 years ago.

When the results came back, the boffin who had done the testing for SBS told me he wanted to meet me personally to give me the results because my mitochondrial DNA (passed to me from Granny Booth) was the most unusual he had ever seen! I was filled with curiosity and not a little trepidation—what could 'unusual' mean, exactly? It turned out my mitochondrial DNA is ancient—100,000 years old. It is called haplotype L1 and is black African. For the 'dilution', as he called it, to have occurred—in other words, for me to look as I do—the introduction of European genes must have happened between 300 and 500 years ago.

In 1500 (or 1700), my African great-great-great-etc-grandmother had a daughter to a white man, who had a daughter to a white man, who had a daughter to a white man, and so on. Of course, I thought of slavery. But who knows? I don't and I never will, but at least I know something about all those grandmothers, one of whom must have been the last to know that particular family secret. I was delighted when both my grandchildren were born and I love them both equally, but I confess to a small secret thrill when my granddaughter was born. My grandson has his mother's mitochondrial DNA, but he cannot pass it on. My granddaughter can bestow that ancient lineage on her children.

To be a grandmother is a privilege and a pleasure. It gives you a chance to be of use to the next generation. It gives you a chance to repay the debt you owe all the grandmothers who came before you and who helped their daughters to be parents long enough for them also to become grandmothers. And I cannot help but feel pleased that, after centuries, that long-lost African grandmother has not had her existence entirely erased. She lives on, in us.

We grandmothers make history, repeat history, carry history and pass on history. We pass on stories, nursery rhymes, family sayings and the unspoken, unacknowledged ripples of long-forgotten events, traumas, twists and turns in our complex lives. Our face, our touch, the sound of our voice, the smell of our skin may be forgotten, but we are there, inside our grand-children. Pass it on.

Auntie Daphne Milward

A Mima's Story

A grandmother has a lot to say. Mima is the name for grandmother in our clan. Everyone should remember it.

Grandmother? I should fling my arms wide when I say *grandmother* because with our people there is a different idea of the word.

I have three grandsons from my two daughters, Karen and Shelley: Kayn, twenty, Christopher, fourteen, and Nicholas, twelve. But I am not just grandmother to my three biological grandchildren, I am a grandmother to so many others in my clan. Family is everything to Aboriginal people. There are circles within circles, but we are all family. I am from the Yorta Yorta Nation, whose country extends throughout the top area of Victoria and some of New South Wales, but within the Yorta Yorta Nation I am a member of a smaller clan, the

Wollithica. All over Australia we have clan groups and larger tribes that belong to the nations of Aboriginal peoples.

Because of my family, my upbringing and what I have experienced, it is natural that I have advocated for my people and I haven't stopped, despite ill health. I am nearly eighty and I've lived a very active life. And a varied one. I once added up all the jobs I have had since I started work at sixteen and it came to twenty-seven. So the changes I've seen are astonishing. My family have always been outspoken and concerned about all the issues of race, discrimination and justice, but these have not always been in the foreground the way they are now. When I was small and living on the banks of the Goulburn River at Mooroopna in Victoria, the concerns of my people were more about simple needs, about survival.

These days I am involved in two educational programs delivered in the early years and school sectors. The first, Cultural Understanding and Safety Training, involves me educating teachers working in early childhood and right through to secondary school levels. The aim is for me to share my cultural and historical knowledge with teachers. I deliver two sessions per school and then the Koorie Education Support Officers advise the teachers where they can access further information (internet, local Aboriginal organisations and networks) to help them work with young Aboriginal people.

The second program involves me visiting kindergartens and primary schools. I tell the children some of the things I know, things I've come to understand over a long life that could not be more different from theirs. It's fun; I enjoy charming the children with stories and illustrations of the country we all live in. Children find it easy to learn how the land is connected to them. I will speak to them if they care to listen; that way they see and hear someone from a culture that is the oldest culture on Earth.

The hardest task is convincing the teachers that what we want to talk about with their students is worthwhile. Some teachers assume that all history is always past and we have arrived at a good place. But people my age have lived it, so we have things to speak about that should be heard, not swept under the rug. The Roman philosopher Cicero once said, 'To be ignorant of the past is to remain a child'—that is so true. The past is not ancient history to me. It is living history. I am living history.

I have a big possum-skin cloak, fifteen possum pelts, which I made myself. On the inside I have drawn my personal dreaming. 'Dreaming is like a totem,' I explain to the children, and they especially love this. I have the long-necked turtle, as well as the dreaming of my clan and some other pictures. It contains the story of my life and is yet to be finished. I like the fact that these possum cloaks are what everyone from my country used in the past. They were everyday things, worn to keep out the cold. They were not ceremonial robes, as people seem to think. The stories and detailed drawings of symbols and pictures on the inside of the cloak show how an individual's lived experience is tied into our cultural connection to country.

The children love to look at my cloak and think about the images on it. They want to know everything. How is it sewn together? How did I make pictures on the inside skin? What do the patterns mean? Where did I learn about them? Of course, I explain that I haven't used the old methods of kangaroo sinew to sew the pelts together, or bones to punch holes in the skin, nor have I used a hot pointed stick and ochre to etch in the drawings, but they love to know how the drawings used to be made. They are also keen to have a personal totem themselves! What they especially love is rolling around in my cloak.

So, in a sense, I am a grandmother to all these children I happen to spend some time with. In our culture the Elders carry the wisdom or the knowledge, all that deep knowledge that has been passed on orally—traditionally we didn't write things down. It is a different way of thinking from that of a written culture. Everything is mapped out in the head.

Grandmothers in all cultures do this: they keep the stories, tell the tales. And the children learn important things they need to know from us, sometimes things that have been passed down through the generations. There is no religion in Aboriginal culture. We believe in a creator who gave us our lore and laws to follow. The laws mainly involve looking after the environment and maintaining our connection to country. You're taught that this is your responsibility, because the land provides for you, not just food, but in all sorts of ways. You need to be taught to listen to the land. If you listen to the lessons properly, you will learn how to live life properly.

The children don't know they are learning as they observe and take in things, as we go about ordinary life and talk about our lived experience. Traditionally, grandmothers have had the time: while the younger, more able people were out working, the older people stayed behind and looked after the babies.

I also belong to a program in schools where we act as substitute grandparents for Aboriginal children who don't have grandparents or anyone who is in a position to act as grandparents. This means going to events at school or occasionally doing things a biological grandparent might do. So, you see, I want to spread my arms wide when I say that word *grandmother*.

My father was English/Australian and, although he acknowledged me, he didn't have anything to do with my upbringing. I am filled, made, created by all those conscious and unconscious things that came from my mother's side. My birth mother was an itinerant worker and had to move a lot, so I went backwards and forwards between my mother and grandmother until I was about five. Most of my family were itinerant and needed to follow the seasonal work of fruit and vegetable picking, but the clan was based in Mooroopna and up near Barmah and Echuca and on the Cummeragunja Reserve. It's complicated, but these threads of family are critically important. And holding these threads in my head is the important part of being a grandmother.

Traditionally, clan groups were family groups, so you didn't have just one set of parents, you had two or three sets of parents. The whole group had responsibility for the children.

If you were crying or had fallen over, any one of the family members would look after you. We were a very close-knit clan and the nurturing was done by everyone. Love was never limited to your own children.

I never felt threatened or afraid as a child. We say that in our community you have many eyes on you. They are always watching what you do. You feel safe.

From the age of five, I lived with my aunt and uncle. They had a permanent house in Mooroopna and were the people who raised me from then on. I called them mum and dad and that's how I've always thought of them. My 'grandmother' was mum's first cousin. My real grandmother was also moving around with the family, so I saw her when she came back for work. But I had other grandmothers, or nanas, and I always felt connected within the family group. As I said, it is complicated!

I was born in 1940, so I grew up with a mixture of contemporary and traditional ways. My family has adapted to modern life, while still keeping some of our ways of life.

The grandmothers are expected to pass on the critical knowledge of family connections. It isn't an exclusive female thing—some men have this knowledge, of course—but now it is the grandmothers, people like me, who know exactly who is who in the complicated network of family threads. I am always being called upon to untangle who someone might be related to. This is often the case with young people who are romantically linked, because in our culture there are very strict rules about intermarriage.

I was there at the birth of Kayn, and I lived with my daughter, Karen, and him until he was about ten years old, so I have been very present in his life. I'm really pleased that I've had a positive influence on his life. We remain close and text with each other, which makes me feel very contemporary. What might be unusual, or different, from mainstream Australian families is that we always welcome family into our homes. No matter how distant the bloodline might be, if they are clan, they are family and they are welcome. If we have a house, it is also their house. When my daughter, Kayn and I were sharing a house, living happily together, there would always be other family members present, so Kayn had many eyes on him.

Of course, if children are to identify as Aboriginal, they need to be taught the old ways and live with the culture, so they know who they are and where they come from. My husband was not Aboriginal, but he was happy for me to expose our children to their culture and to the things that were extremely important to me. I find it harder to be this sort of grandmother with my second daughter Shelley's two boys, who live up in Brisbane. When children are small, however, it tends to be easier to teach them. But we never force our children or our grandchildren into being fully involved in Aboriginal issues. They need to know enough to be able to make choices and respond in the right way to Aboriginal issues in today's society, but they can't make choices if they are ignorant.

It is difficult to describe, but I need to elaborate on what it means when our culture has more than one grandmother per child. Imagine a grandmother who is not that woman who has a commanding influence, or who is there simply to bestow material gifts on a few grandchildren. I am talking, of course, about a certain stereotype of a grandma that you see in the media—one who is more like a fairy godmother than a practical woman (although I think there is more call these days for grandmothers to be practical, because their children are often working). My idea of 'bestowing' is to give my grandchildren access to the culture, the old ways and, most importantly, if possible, some of the language. We cannot lose what language we have. We need to teach the children that English is not their first language. I see all around me how the old ways are breaking down, and this brings an urgency to my grand-mothering.

We clans all live apart now. In the old days we lived together, all of us, even in the bush. But it was a terrible time for our people back then, especially in terms of health care problems. We were hired out as casual workers but, as everyone now knows, we were not paid. Our money went into a fund established through the Aborigines Welfare Board. And you need to know that we were not counted in any census, until the 1967 referendum approved changes to the Constitution. And it was not until 1965 that all Indigenous Australians had the right to vote in both state and federal elections. And among the many areas we were denied access to was higher education.

So in 1939, half the people in my clan, over 150 of them,

walked off the Cummeragunja Reserve in New South Wales. This was the first time my people had rebelled against the way we were made to live. The Cummeragunja Walk-Off is extremely significant in our history. Although I wasn't born until the following year, it had a profound effect on my life. The walk-off was a way of showing that we were not powerless. Some of the clan went to Echuca and others went to Mooroopna and Shepparton, where they camped on the banks of the Goulburn.

We used to live on the river flats between Mooroopna and Shepparton. You had to get this thing called an Exemption Certificate issued by the government and only then were you allowed off the reserve to go and find work. You could live in town without police supervision, but there were curfews and a lot of discrimination. So when people got exemptions they started living on the fringes of towns. That's why they got to be known as 'fringe dwellers'. I was only four, but I have very clear memories of living as one of the fringe dwellers on the river flats between Mooroopna and Shepparton. This is all recent history and it should not be overlooked or forgotten. Over the past few years some of the best knowledge of our history and inter-racial relations has come from accounts in reports written by the government body, the Aborigines Welfare Board, as well as from accounts in diaries of settlers, explorers and others. They are very straightforward accounts and add to our knowledge—particularly to my knowledge when I talk to my grandchildren and when I talk in schools.

People tell me I have confidence. I can only think that this confidence comes from belonging to a prominent clan, and from our connection with other prominent clans. We were always spokespersons for our people. Our Elders, William Cooper and William Ferguson, Pastor Douglas Nicholls, Jack Patton, Marg Tucker, Geraldine Briggs, Amy Cooper, Gladys Nicholls and Nora Charles, were always interested in building up a stronger voice for our people. When I first came to Melbourne, I worked for the Aborigines Advancement League with Pastor Doug Nicholls, Aunty Gladys, his wife, and Stan Davey. And I was lucky. I was not traumatised by being taken away from my family by the authorities, or by being sent to a foster home. Sadly, the lives of many of my family members have been shaped by this sort of trauma of separation.

I think it is interesting that a little girl born in Mooroopna, who grew up in those shacks on the area known as 'The Flats', those tumbles of tin and wood scavenged from the local tip not far from us, who was encouraged to leave school at fourteen, stayed at school until sixteen. I can only put it down to the strength of the clan, men as well as women: they gave me the confidence never to doubt myself.

In the past, as white settlement increased and our land was taken, conflicts arose and it was always the men speaking to the men. We tend not to think about this, but that was the way it was. The white women settlers didn't have voices— their husbands would do the talking—and it was the same with the Aboriginal people. Men like to speak to men.

In the 1940s, following the Cummeragunja Walk-Off,

things started to change. For many different social and cultural reasons, and especially because of the Second World War, Aboriginal women, women like my mum, started to speak out. The world had shifted and they found their voices, you could say. The men seemed discouraged, so what else could the women do? The women needed to speak out for themselves and for their children about the important issues. It was the women who were the strongest voices, who were keeping the old ways and keeping families together. I have to be delicate talking about this. Traditionally, there was women's business and men's business and they would come together to discuss Aboriginal affairs and issues. Together they would plan for the whole group. But over time, the men seem to have become drawn into destructive behaviour. Or they have become dispirited.

My mum was involved in forming a group in Mooroopna to talk with the local council and officials. We had a lot of help from the Save the Children Fund and from the unions. They were extraordinary in their practical and political help at various times. My mum worked with a marvellous woman called Sister Turner, from the Save the Children Fund, and they set up a kindergarten on the river. Because everyone was moving around, it was difficult to get a basic education, but the mums realised how important this was. These women set the example for me; they were my role models. Our history is colourful and we have a lot to be proud of—and we need to speak about it, not just as grandmothers, but as people who have this knowledge of a particular world to pass on.

The important thing for me now is to tell Kayn—the grandson I see most of, because he lives closer—about who his family is, to enable him to see himself within this small circle, and then the wider circle of family, his connection to both the Gunnai/Kurnai and the Yorta Yorta Nations. I also want him to know about some of the old ways, even though they might not seem that important to a young man in a modern world. I want him to know about the welcome ceremonies, the smoking ceremonies, to learn some language. He knows how to acknowledge the Traditional Owners of the Land, wherever he may be. He did an awesome acknowledgement of country at our NAIDOC event a few years ago and again at the opening of a new building for his scouts group. He knows his totems, penguin and turtle, and he participated in burning symbols of his message onto a possum-skin pelt to say goodbye to a dear Aboriginal friend who wanted to be buried in her cloak. If he knows who he is and is responsible about that knowledge, he can start to give back to the community. Kayn already knows a lot about his connections all over Australia.

I am proud that I have been able to impart some of my traditional cultural knowledge to Kayn, and that he has become a strong and resilient young Aboriginal man. He also makes sure that I am okay, and comes to check in on me, staying overnight occasionally and asking me questions about our culture and identity.

But there is the wider perspective too. It isn't just for Kayn and my other grandchildren. I would like to be able to pass on whatever knowledge I have of those more than sixty thousand years of a lived culture on this country to other children as well, Aboriginal and non-Aboriginal. There is so much to know. This is why I am working with educators, and this is why I made the possum-skin cloak. If you teach children at this very intimate level, you can help to prevent racism, which seems to me to be based on nothing but ignorance. Children walk in the footprints of their Elders so they can be strong in their cultural identity and have connection to history, culture and who they truly are.

Glenda Guest

GR and Me

She is eight years old. She is tall and thin. Her arms and legs are long. Good coordination is yet to be achieved. She has dark brown eyes and olive skin. Her hair is long, black and curly.

I met her in Chicago, a squalling bundle of energy who, for this story, I'll call GR. Her mother, my daughter, had been in a birthing suite at Chicago University Medical Centre for thirty-six gruelling hours with pre-eclampsia, a baby who did not want to be born, and a severe asthma attack due to the stress of it all. In the tense minutes following birth, GR's medical team forced her to deal with the world. She clearly did not much like what she saw and expressed herself with an ear-piercing wail of outrage. 'Give her to her grandmother,' a nurse said. The sudden quiet made the medicos look up but GR and I took no notice: we were having a getting-to-know-you spiritual moment gazing into each other's eyes. I thought she said, *I know you.*

Four years later, I told her: 'When you were born you looked into my eyes and said, "I know you."'

'Could I talk already?' the child-of-practical-mind replied.

During the four years after her birth, I saw GR only twice before the family came back to Australia: country New South Wales to Chicago is over half a world away in more than one respect. We met in Sorrento, Italy, for five days, when she was two and a half, and a small connection was forged, but she was so supervised by her parents and so attached to her father there was little room in her life for extra people at that time.

The next time was the day they returned to Australia. They were last off the plane, this small family. We watched them walk past the windows in the off-ramp, my daughter and son-in-law carrying the things needed for a twenty-four-hour trip with a four-year-old. As they rounded the bend into the empty arrivals hall, GR saw us waiting, her grandfather almost hidden by a giant white teddy bear, and she practically flew towards us. I dropped down to her level and propped myself against her grandfather's leg; even then her momentum almost knocked me over. So there we were, all hugged up, and she didn't know how to disengage. *Why don't you say hello to Grandpa now* gave her permission to let go.

Other people's expectations can, at times, get in the way of forging relationships. Until I had my own daughter, forty years ago, I'd had little to do with babies or toddlers, and I still don't find them interesting. 'Play with her,' GR's parents urged. 'I don't play with babies,' I said, and a small rift opened.

When GR and her parents returned to Australia, they stayed with us for a couple of weeks. Was I an instant grand-mother? I tried, but the child was unknown territory. There was also, with the best of intentions, arbitration between GR and myself and I found I rather resented being manipulated into doing things not of my own choosing. The dinner table was dominated by a shrill, loud, young voice that was encour-aged to speak, but which did not form words clearly at times, and the child was always the focus of attention.

My own granddaughter-hood was with a strict middle-England Methodist grandmother who, I know, loved me dearly, but believed the child was part of a family, not the centre; as did my own mother; as do I.

I believe this for more than one reason, but the main one is that if, in a family, all the attention goes to the child, the main relationship cannot help but be compromised. When the child—particularly an only child who does not have to share attention with siblings—is always prioritised, what happens to the vital relationship between the parents? How does the child understand and learn about kind and loving relationships that do not focus solely on her/himself? The parents' relationship is the basis on which the child, when an adult, will model their own emotional life; she/he must be able to see their day-to-day affectionate and caring interaction and know this is love.

I was caring for GR not long after they came back to Australia, as her mother was working in the USA for three months and commuting every few weeks to have time at home. Her father worked full-time, so I filled the gap for a while.

I wondered why she wanted to watch me dress or shower, then realised there had been no older people in her life so far, and she had never seen an ageing body. She was fascinated by my breasts and her hand crept out, then pulled back. 'You can touch if you want to,' I said. She did.

'Does it feel like Mumma's?' It did.

Her finger traced the nipple areola. But that didn't.

'Thank you, Glennie,' she said, and giggled, very aware that this was stretching personal contact boundaries.

'You're welcome.'

Her interest in my body continued for some time.

'Let me see your teeth,' she said, and I gave her a big smile.

'Why aren't they really white?'

'Your teeth get old too,' I said. 'They can change colour.'

She touched the spot under my chin, fascinated by its softness.

'Please don't do that, GR.'

'Why?'

'Because I don't like it and I want you to stop.'

She understood that reason; being in control of your own body and not letting someone touch it if you didn't want it was already ingrained in her awareness of herself.

Those weeks of caring for GR were an eye-opener for me. Wisely, her parents had enrolled her in childcare for a few hours most weekdays. Even so, being one-on-one with a little person I didn't know was challenging: the move to a new country and her mother's absence for two or three weeks at a time meant she was highly vulnerable. I found an early bath, and lots of stuff to play with in the water, was useful. I planned as many outings as were possible in Canberra in summer—movies, a kids' event at the War Memorial, a couple of live-theatre shows for preschoolers.

Walking from the car park to the theatre one day, I realised we hadn't talked about what to do if we were separated for whatever reason. We sat down on a street bench.

'GR, what would you do if you couldn't find me in a crowd of people?'

Silence. Thinking. 'I'd ask an adult to find you.'

'Just any adult?'

'No. A policeman. Or another lady.'

'Okay. But how would they know who to look for?'

More thinking. 'I'd tell them you're wearing black jeans and a white shirt.'

'Like that?' I pointed to a young girl walking past wearing a David Jones uniform.

'No-o! I'd say that you have very white hair and are very, very old!'

So that was sorted, then! And I completely understood that, to a four-year-old child, I was indeed very, very old.

'I really must remember to bring my walking stick next time.'

'You don't use a walking stick, silly Glennie,' the practical child said.

'No, I don't. I was just joking.'

'But that's not funny.'

The turning point of acceptance came after I'd been at her house for a week.

Each morning she didn't want her father to leave for work, but on this day it was particularly difficult for him to get out the door. There was much crying and hanging onto him by GR, until I said, 'Just go. I'll take care of it.'

She stood on the balcony screaming, 'Don't go, Daddy, don't go!' as he rode his bicycle down the road. How hard it must have been for him to keep pedalling. How abandoned she must have felt at that moment. I picked her up, lifted her inside (no mean feat considering her height and my lack of such) and shut the door.

'It's really tough sometimes, isn't it, when someone has to leave and you don't want them to.'

Her reaction surprised me. She threw herself onto me and clung on, but the emotion gradually abated and we talked a little about leaving and returning: 'He always comes home at night, doesn't he?' I realised that I was not only referring to her father going to work for the day, but to her mother, who had commitments in another country that had to be fulfilled. For a child, the two to three weeks away each time must have seemed a lifetime. 'And Mumma, she will always come home, even though it seems to be a long time. I promise you she will.'

'Pinky-promise,' she said, and we solemnly hooked little fingers. I knew this was a promise I could keep.

She was fine with a different discipline from what she was used to. I was much more lenient in some things and tougher in others.

Walking in the city one day, I could see her shoes were hurting her. 'Take them off and carry them,' I said.

'I can take them off?'

'Sure.'

'Really?'

'Yes. Just watch where you walk.' And she skipped along the hot pavement with bare feet, doing ballet poses.

The other side:

'GR, please put away all the stuff you took out of the cupboard. Now, please, before dinner.'

A reluctant crawl towards a room of chaos, and an attempt at negotiation from this stubborn Taurus kid.

'I'll do this bit, and you can do that over there.'

'GR, you made the mess, and it's your responsibility to clean it up.'

'But we have to help each other!'

This was a tough one: how to teach responsibility and helpfulness at the same time?

'I'm helping by making your dinner. So, do you want to eat or do you want me to help put things away?'

She actually considered these alternatives, and I prepared myself to let her go to bed unfed, but she decided food was the better choice. My credo of carrying through something I have set up obviously needs more thought when giving choices!

On a hot day in Canberra, that first summer after they returned, my daughter and I were in the back garden, where GR was 'going nudey' under the sprinkler spray. She went inside to get my hat for me, then bounced back down the steps into the garden; her tall body and thin legs and arms making her look like a flying stick insect. The Akubra hat on her head was the only thing she was wearing and her long black curls flew around it. '*Yippy-ai-ah!*' she shouted. '*Yippy-ai-oh!*'

That this child had nothing to do with older people for her first four years showed in various ways. She had to talk herself, several times, through the concept of Momma having a mother, obviously finding it unbelievable. And it took a little longer for her to accept that Momma's momma also had one, even though she had died. Old photos helped. But once she grasped the reality—

The phone rang quite early one morning.

'Glennie! Glennie!'

'Hi, GR. What's up?'

'Momma just said bugger.'

'Ohhhh. Really. Bad Mumma. Why are you telling me?'

'Well, you're her momma. You should do something.'

Daughter in the background: 'You're getting me into trouble.'

GR to her mother: 'That's what kids do.'

And then there's GR's grandfather, a quiet, diffident man who should have many children who have many children of their own, a man whose life should revolve around family, but to whom fate gave one child, who had one child herself.

In many ways he is a traditional grandfather, wanting a grandchild who will visit him in his workshop and be interested in making things. He wants a close relationship with this rather unusual child. He takes her to school when he's in town and, on the first time, GR introduced him to her teacher, which made him happy. He has picked her up from preschool and school on occasions.

He leaves chocolate frogs in the fridge whenever he goes to her house; when she occasionally visits us, he takes her to the beach sometimes. He tells her dad-jokes, but because she doesn't understand them she finds them rather disconcerting and maybe a bit threatening. She's not used to adults joking around with her, saying things that aren't real.

I would like her to go to him first when we arrive at her home, for him to be the one to make her smile. Even so, there is the beginning of a relationship there, but one, I fear, that is difficult at a distance and that may slip away unless nurtured. I hope, for them both, that does not happen; they need each other in a relationship that is different from any other either of them will ever have.

She is eight years old now. Her mind is always moving. Full and detailed information is her mind-food. She analyses answers until she understands, and then applies them to other situations, most times correctly. Friends and family could find her bossy. The books she reads would challenge a twelve-year-old child. She asks for mathematics and science problems to do, for fun.

GR started asking questions that seemed too complex for her age before she started preschool, where her mission in life was to organise the class at anytime, anywhere. Her mother said she seemed ahead of her age markers. And what could she do about her bossiness with other kids, she wondered. Apparently I replied, 'What do you expect? Two pit bulls don't breed a chihuahua.'

I imagine the person she will be when her huge IQ and her burgeoning EQ meet and become complementary. I imagine a person who is strong and a bit wild, who—as long as she has a firm home base—sees the world as her oyster, who understands that her privilege comes with responsibility to the world and acts on it. Who, because she understands herself, understands others. Why do I imagine such a person? Because she wrote this at school:

The Best Part of Me.

The best part of me is my heart. When I feel sad my heart makes me happy again. It holds my greatest secrets and is full of love. My heart makes me feel brave when I am scared. My heart is the best thing anyone could wish for. I care for my heart more than ever.

My greatest wish for her is not academic or professional achievement, for that will come anyway, but that she will understand other people's hearts.

It's not possible to have a close relationship at a distance, at first half a world away during those vital, bonding early years, now three hours' drive between homes, which means—between school, parents working, everyone's commitments—there is still not a great deal of contact, certainly not the easy, day-to-day dropping in to each other's homes that is part of an extended family life. I feel GR considers us, her grandfather and me, not so much as family, but rather as people who happen to be around at times, even though, intellectually, she understands the connection.

Her mother keeps me in GR's life by talking about me to her, and not letting the relationship slide away from the child's consciousness. We occasionally talk by phone, but there is no landline in their house and GR has to use her mother's or father's iPhone on loudspeaker. There is no chance for a one-on-one conversation.

Even so, given that we only saw each other twice before she was four and maybe four or five times a year, briefly, since her life in Australia, we do okay most of the time.

They change so quickly, children, when you see them rarely. There she was in the birthing suite, a screaming bundle of outrage. Turn around and she's flying down the entry tunnel at the airport. Turn around twice, a photo pings into my

iPhone messages and she is in her uniform on that momentous first day of formal schooling. Turn again and she's in
Grade Two with extension classes for children who are ahead
in maths and reading.

GR: 'When are you going to die?'

'Don't really know. We don't know that. Why do you ask?'
(Always a good idea to get the motivation.)

GR: 'Well, you have to be a hundred to die. I just want to
know so I can be ready.'

'Ready for what?'

GR: 'Ready to be sad.'

The difference now between the generations is probably more
pronounced than at any time in history, and my generation
of women is partly responsible, in that we told our daughters
they could do anything, have it all. My heart bends when I
watch my own daughter managing a demanding career that
she loves, the home stuff, the child's stuff, and little or nothing
of her own stuff. We surely realise now that we have done our
girls a grave disservice as we watch them juggling the 'it all'
of work and family, with little time for self-care and social
contact, and, sometimes, compensatory overzealous parenting.
Michelle Obama called it correctly when she said, 'So you can
have it all? Nope, not at the same time.' If the grandmothers
are around, they pick up the slack and care for the grandkids, often to the detriment of their own lives. But maybe the
problem, if we view it as such, is of our own making.

I don't have that decision to make about how much to help with the one and only grandchild—we live too far apart. Would I take on that responsibility, if needed? Maybe. Maybe not. Probably. Of course.

I watch in admiration as her parents prepare her for adulthood in a world that will be unrecognisable to my generation: setting boundaries of behaviour that are strongly kept to, making her realise that some things may come easily for her but that she has to try, and keep on trying, when they don't. Even so, I want to pick her up, give her a make-your-own-fun childhood, let her wildness run free, let her develop however it happens—but that world has passed and I can only do what I have already done:

'You can phone me any time at all, GR. Any time, even if you just want to say hello and hang up.'

'Any time? Even in the middle of the night?'

'Any time at all. I will always answer, no matter where I am in the world. Pinky-promise.'

Elizabeth Chong

At Por Por's Table

Being a grandmother doesn't change who you are: a daughter, a sister, an aunt, a wife, a mother. But the new role brings a different perspective on how you see yourself. Or how others may see you.

Does the title *grandmother* suddenly make one feel older, and look older to the world? Yes, it probably does. It conjures up the stereotypical picture-book image of a grandmother— you know the one I mean—a small, bespectacled, white-haired woman in a rocking chair, shawl over her shoulders, rug over knees and knitting needles on her lap. An idealised image of the perfect, meek and mild grandmother—a woman with her real life behind her.

If this is everybody's idea of a perfect grandmother, then I, and millions of other grandmothers, fall down badly. I am the perfect opposite to that little lady: I do not own a rocking chair and my hair is not white because I have it coloured at the hairdresser's regularly. I do, however, admit to a warm rug over my knees at night, and I *can* knit.

I used to knit socks and jumpers for my children, but as a grandmother I have no time to knit for my grandchildren. I am a working grandmother and I am not home long enough to pick up knitting needles. And really, who has time to wash woollen socks or woollen jumpers these days? A live-in grandmother, perhaps, or that woman with the rocking chair. Certainly not me.

The world has changed, and families have adapted and changed with it. For me, there are no rules, no code to follow about being a grandmother. It simply means that I am there for all my children, grandchildren and great-grandchildren, to give them my unconditional love, encouragement and support in whatever way I can, and so that they know how precious they are to me. By my presence and example in their lives, I hope each grandchild may have been inspired and motivated to be the best person they can be, to contribute to the wider world in their own way. I never wished to impose my expectations on them. I feel very strongly about this and have never lectured or instructed my grandchildren to follow a particular direction. Being there, being available, is enough.

On a more practical level, I cook for them. It is expected of me and I am entirely happy to comply. There have been countless wonderful meals shared by my entire family over many years, celebrating many milestones. The grandchildren are very familiar with sitting at Por Por's (Cantonese for grand-mother) table and eating my signature dishes. They know I will make a special effort to cook their favourites: traditional Chinese soups made from pure chicken stock, studded with special ingredients like lotus root, lily buds, red dates, goji berries, dried fungi and shiitake mushrooms. These soups have been passed down to me from my mother and my grand-mother, but I wonder if they will survive down the generations of Chinese Australians so removed from their ancestors?

Chinese culture and traditional Chinese cuisine may be lost or diluted in the passage of time, but the love and respect for the food of their childhood will always have a strong pull for my children and grandchildren, and they come back 'home' to it time and time again. I know some traditional dishes have been passed on to them, because their own meals sometimes resemble mine. My celebrated roast chicken (cooked at every birthday), steamed fish with ginger and shallots, steamed egg custard and braised potato with Chinese bacon, beef and vege-table stir-fry—all these dishes now share the table with pasta and pizza.

I have raised four children, so feel pretty qualified to offer advice on how to care for babies and how to rear children. But, being a wise and loving grandmother, I usually refrain from doing so. With each new generation, there are new rules and regulations. Over my long life, I have seen, often with amazement, that what was once decreed to be the right and only way to care for babies and children has become wrong and outmoded. And, of course, it is so tempting to say 'in my day...', but I stop myself because I remember how differently I brought up my own babies compared to the way my mother brought up her brood of six.

•

When I am with my grandchildren, I marvel at the natural warmth and easy relationship I have with them, as opposed to the formal relationship I had with my own grandmother so long ago. According to traditional Chinese beliefs, old people are respected and revered. The young have yet to prove themselves and earn respect. I not sure that this is still the case in modern China, but perhaps these ways are still adhered to in the countryside.

I never knew my maternal grandmother, as she was unable to leave China under communist rule, and died in Hong Kong shortly after my father finally obtained a visa for her to come to Australia.

But I still have vivid memories of my paternal grandmother, from over eighty years ago. Grandma arrived from a village in southern China in 1934 with my mother, my sisters, my brother and me, aged three. Grandma lived with us until I was eight years old, after which she moved between our family and my uncles' and aunties' families. We were all closely involved in each other's lives, as a typical Chinese extended family, and it was impossible to imagine life without Grandma.

Like me, my grandmother did not fit the Anglo picture-book image of the perfect grandmother. She was a feisty woman who lived by the Confucian philosophy that the old are to be revered by the young, that the younger generations take over all cares and burdens, making every effort to ensure for the comfort of the old. Consequently, Grandma expected those around her to do her bidding, and she was not willing to put up with nonsense from her grandchildren. In keeping with Chinese tradition, she was the honoured matriarch of the family, and her four sons, and especially her daughters-in-law, made sure she wanted for nothing. Her grandchildren were in awe of her. She certainly wasn't the cuddly type. She would tell us stories about life back in China, how bandits would attack and the villagers would run into the hills for safety. But even when she issued a warning to us of the consequences of bad behaviour, I think we still sometimes took her words with a grain of salt.

Grandma was a diminutive figure, barely five feet tall. Her grey hair was tied back in a little bun at the nape of her neck, and she mostly wore a Chinese black silk trouser suit, or a black silk Chinese dress for more formal occasions. At home, she wore black, embroidered cloth shoes, encasing her tiny feet, which had been deformed from foot-binding when she was a young girl.

I was one of her twenty-three grandchildren, but my sisters and brother and I knew her better than my cousins did, as she had lived longer with us. She taught me how to knit during the Second World War. Japan had just attacked China and everyone in the overseas Chinese community in Australia threw themselves into the war effort through benefit concerts, food parcels, and knitted scarves and rugs for the soldiers. Grandma was the expert in our family: she taught my sisters and me to knit little squares out of different coloured skeins of wool, then my aunts would dutifully sew the squares together into rugs. Once there was a great furor when it was discovered that some naughty person had cut up all the squares that had just been carefully sewn together. Grandma guessed who that naughty person was, but I was thankful she never let on.

I also learnt from Grandma how to cook her favourite dish, beef and tomatoes, which I still cook today exactly as she taught me. Her recipe differs from other recipes of this dish I have seen. One of the major differences was that she always used ground beef, not finely sliced rump steak. I think now it may have been because Grandma found it easier to eat ground beef. I also imagine that Grandma was cooking dishes like this based on memories of village life in China, and that she had, over the years, re-created them to suit a different time and a different place.

A lovely memory I have of Grandma is her love of flowers. At that time, we lived near the Queen Victoria Market in Melbourne, above a shop and factory. We were surrounded by concrete, but that did not stop my tiny Grandma from exercising her green thumb. In the cracks of the concrete driveway she planted seedlings, her favourite pansies and marigolds. The scents of her flowers, the smells of her cooking, all remain with me so strongly that I can instantly transport myself back with my grandmother. But if I were to name her real legacy, I would say it was her insistence on politeness and respect when addressing people, particularly those older than ourselves.

Grandma was adamant that we address our elders properly. The Chinese have titles for everyone—grandmother on your father's side, fourth-youngest uncle, second-oldest aunt, eldest sister, younger brother and so on. Everyone must be greeted according to their standing in the hierarchy of the family and society. Even siblings are given titles. I was called third elder sister by Chinese friends outside the family, as I am the third girl in my family of six children. Even older friends or associates of the family are called uncle or aunt. To ignore this protocol and simply say 'hello' to relatives or to others is a gross error, an insult, and in my childhood would always invite the sternest rebuke from my parents or grandparents. I once did slip up, and I have never forgotten my grandmother's reprimands. These days, when I hear a casual 'hello' in the Western manner from a young person to an older person, without the correct title, I still shudder in horror. The power of what my grandmother would think is still uppermost in my mind.

Nevertheless, it was inevitable that my life as an Australian girl outside of my Chinese home would have a huge influence on my outlook and habits. Unlike my grandmother, I am not held in awe as the family matriarch, nor do I expect or want that kind of status. I hold onto my independence fiercely, including my financial independence. I do not expect my children to do my bidding, although I do appreciate it if any of them offer help.

It is not the Chinese way to show or display affection, not

even to one's children and grandchildren. We grandchildren did not have an intimate relationship with Grandma; I do not remember any display of affection from her, no hugs, and especially no kisses. I remember feeling uncomfortable and embarrassed when my Australian girlfriends exchanged hugs and kisses with their parents and grandparents in public. I had never seen this before, and I thought how wonderful it was to be so free.

The Chinese of my generation view any public display of emotion or affection as inappropriate and distasteful. My own mother would show her love for me not with a hug or a kiss, but by cooking a special dish for my birthday, and I knew that the extra piece of roast pork or dumpling given to me was evidence that I was loved. That was enough. In Chinese culture, which had often been defined by famine, food assumes particular importance. Food can, indeed, equal love.

In my own life, I admit I have a little of that Chinese distaste for public shows of affection but, thank God, I have no hesitation when it comes to my own grandchildren and I give them lots of hugs and kisses. My five grandchildren know that I love them all dearly, in spite of the fact that I have never been an available, babysitting grandmother.

For most of my life I have been a working woman, and have not had the luxury of many free days or nights, so babysitting has simply not been on my agenda. My grandchildren inherited a working grandmother who could hardly find time for herself, let alone care for them. My children, Michael, Katrina, Andrea and Richard, have always been excellent parents, and have always known and accepted that I had to be a working mum, and then a working grandmother. They understood that I could not be on call for babysitting duties. I don't know if this was a disappointment to them, but if this was the case, they never showed it in any way. And I have not allowed myself to feel overly guilty that I was not sharing the responsibility of raising their children. I could not be a mother all over again.

·

I became a grandmother with the birth of Gabrielle in 1982. Four more grandchildren followed: three beautiful girls, Fiona, Jessica and Teresa, and a wonderful boy, Jai. With each birth, I felt joy, pride and gratitude that these little miracles were a part of our family, as I did with the births of Felicity and Theodore, my great-grandchildren—the bonds that tie are just as strong as when my children were born.

I have grown to enjoy the title of grandmother. In fact the position is rather an exalted one: 'big' is one thing, but when big becomes bigger and more important, then it is 'grand'! So I can be forgiven for being delighted when each grandchild is born and my title becomes even more significant. The new mother and father are usually overwhelmed with the care of their new baby, whereas I can shower unconditional love, free of the stress of responsibility. It is a new and perfect luxury, an unexpected and mysterious thing, but there is no denying the sense of belonging, the sense of continuity when you cradle one of your newborn grandchildren or great-grandchildren who have the same bloodline as yourself. Is DNA the reason for that deep emotional pull that is at once protective and possessive, full of pride and humility?

I know that each grandmother's experience is unique and there are as many different types of grandmothers as there are grains of rice. Some grandmothers, lonely now that their own children have grown up, become mothers again; they cannot wait to do it all once more. These grandmothers are there for their grandchildren 24/7. What a boon for working parents, knowing their little ones are being cared for by their own mothers, knowing they are safe and secure in a family environment.

In these cases, everyone benefits: the young parents can keep their jobs (in most cases, out of sheer necessity) and that wonderful bond between grandmother and grandchild is established, a close and a unique relationship that will last forever.

And yet I am troubled by another side to this arrangement, that of the grandmother taking on again the motherly duties she performed many years ago. In old China, certainly not today, families of two generations lived together under one roof, including the unmarried sister or aunt, who was also a part of the household. Household duties were shared by all members of the family, and the children were cared for by everyone. In that other world, that other time, a grandmother did not have interests of her own. Her life was focused on her family, and she would have been mystified if someone had suggested that she needed her own time and space.

A grandmother has other burdens and it does not seem right to me that she should repeat her life in this way, mothering, unless she truly wants to do it all over again. Nature has decreed that women over a certain age cannot bear children. I am sure this is because nature also knows that women at a certain age do not have the emotional or physical strength and stamina to look after babies and small children full-time.

There is a great deal of pressure on young couples, who may be saving to buy their first home, keeping up payments on a mortgage, running a car, maintaining a certain lifestyle. With the arrival of a baby, the demands increase, so how do the new parents continue to have it all? Often it is simply assumed that grandmothers are around with time on their hands, that they will be besotted with the children, and that they will be happy to give up some of their days for child-minding.

Sometimes a grandmother might be willing, without realising that the physical demands on her body are too much. She is reluctant to tell her daughter or son, and let them down, and so, as usual, she soldiers on. This is a common scenario these days. I do admire those grandmothers who can do it.

My grandchildren have grown into beautiful young adults. While leading different lives, they are all similar threads in the tapestry of our family. Not so long ago those threads were all in China. We must remember that. I am one of the lucky ones who can tell a happy story—my immigrant parents settled in Australia and made a good life here for themselves and their children and contributed a lot to their new society. They gave us the best of both worlds. More than that, they gave us a strong set of values, of fairness and kindness. In turn, I have tried to instil those values in my own children and grandchildren, who contribute to life in this country with love and integrity. I am so proud of them all.

My grandchildren will not remember their grandmother as a little white-haired lady rocking gently in a chair. I hope they will remember her as someone who has inspired them to celebrate life in all its richness, and to never forget to give thanks for all the goodness that is theirs.

Alison Lester

The Very Noisy Grandmother

I'm standing in the takeaway queue in a fancy Indian restaurant. It's busy; all the tables are packed, waiters shooting around with loaded trays. I scan the interior and my gaze comes to rest on the mirror behind the counter. There I am, a tired-looking old bag, dirty hair pulled back in a ponytail, no make-up. And then I see in the reflection that people are staring at me, well, staring at my legs, nudging each other and smiling. I look down. Orange tracksuit pants tucked into black cowboy boots. That'll do it.

And it kind of says everything about me as a grandmother: no time for hair and make-up, jeans off and trackies on because being down on the floor with the kids is no place for tight pants. And cowboy boots because that's all I could find when I volunteered to go with my son Lach to pick up the takeaway. Then when he couldn't get a park it was me jumping out in the rain, me paying, and now me waiting in line, getting laughed at. I'm laughing inside too; it's a pretty funny look.

Before we had this explosion of grandkids, I imagined I'd be a kindly, generous, sweet, venerated grandma, but I'm really more of a loved slave, so busy I hardly have time to ride my horse.

There are three families.

Will and Sam with their four under five, Eddy, Frank, Hattie and Winnie—they can always do with a hand. The energy that comes off those kids is incredible. They came to stay a while ago and when they left every picture in the house was crooked, even the ones up high.

Then there's Clair and Troy with Trixie and Max, also with busy lives. When Trix was a baby, she was so loud she inspired one of my picture books, *The Very Noisy Baby*. But Max is even louder, so sweet you could eat him up, but with a bellow like a bull if the slightest thing is not right. He'll scream the house down at four-thirty a.m, then smile at you when you go into his room. Last time he came to stay, five of the other grandkids were asleep. I didn't want him to wake them, so I took him for a drive at five a.m. There I was in my PJs with a coat over the top, hoping I wouldn't break down or hit a kangaroo on our lonely gravel road.

And Lachie and Georgia have Francesca, with her wicked sense of humour, her striking resemblance to her father (it's very unnerving seeing a six-foot-five man reflected in a baby girl) and a traumatic start in life that has us all weeping whenever we look at her baby photos. She was born ten weeks early and then spent three months in ICU, very ill, undergoing various operations. I felt myself disintegrating as I watched this tiny person, paler than her sheets, fighting for breath. And I am so proud of Lachie and Georgia for being the amazing parents they are, sitting with Francesca day after day, until finally she could come home—with oxygen and a breathing monitor. That was terrifying too. There have been several visits to Emergency, but she's sailing along now, getting bigger, saying more words, just one of the kids. So much that, when she wouldn't have an afternoon nap a few weeks ago, I found myself muttering (I'm deeply ashamed to say), 'Jeez, you're a pain in the arse, Francesca.' She really is one of the gang now.

•

My parents started late and I'm the youngest in my family, so I pretty much missed out on grandmothers. I have a faint memory of Mum's mother frightening me when she joked about having me for dinner.

When my own three children were small, I found it a mixture of delight and frustration. I loved days at home with them—mucking around in the garden, making playdough, playing with puppies, doing all that stuff you do with little kids—but I also thought it was the hardest thing I'd ever done. As soon as I could, I found work that would give me an excuse to have some days off from full-time parenting. This was bliss, a few days at home to hang around with them, and other days when they were cared for by someone else and I went to work, to write and illustrate picture books. Work seemed like a holiday.

My mother was a fabulous grandmother. Nan, the kids called her, and they loved her for her endless patience, full biscuit tins and non-judgemental love. I guess she's the grandmother I thought I'd be, but I'm more like my husband's mother, Grandma Joan, who treated her grandchildren like small adults and delighted them with her ability to swear with a posh accent, usually in the car.

Looking back now, it's as if my time as the mother of babies and little kids only lasted a few years, before they were off at school, then away studying. Next thing, all three were out of the country, and then they came home and teamed up with lovely partners. But I had to wait a while before I become a grandmother. I used to joke that, once the first baby arrived, there'd be an avalanche—that they'd all get onto it. And, sure enough, that's what happened. Will and Sam had baby Eddy, and in the space of four years there were suddenly seven grandchildren.

When I was trying to persuade them to have babies, I said I'd retire and look after the grandchildren five days a week. And I meant it. But when it came to the crunch, I couldn't give up work altogether. Even though I love them dearly, it drives me crazy if I am babysitting all time. It has me on the road a lot, leaving home at five-thirty a.m. to beat the peak hour rush and waiting until six-thirty p.m. to miss the traffic again on the way home. The days can be long when you are on your own with small children and the last hour, dinner and bath-time (the hour from hell), when all of us are tired, can be really exhausting. A glass of wine is sometimes the only thing that gets me over the line.

For a couple of years, Clair lived just around the corner from Lachie, so I looked after Francesca on Clair's day off; that way we could share the kids. It was a nice way of spending time together. One great thing about the grandchildren being so close in age is that they all get on. In fact they LOVE each other, which is a beautiful thing. When they are all at our place together, it's like a little posse on the move: out on the deck, back in the kitchen, then into our bedroom, playing with my shoes and the money jar.

•

A few years ago, before the grandchildren, I was giving a talk about my books, and about kids, and I said how much I used to yell when my kids were little, but that I hadn't yelled for years, that I couldn't imagine getting angry enough to yell about anything. Well, that's changed. If I'm having to get a whole lot of things done, I find myself bellowing. 'Get in this bath now!' 'Come here!' 'Put your hat on!' And when I really do my block, I am embarrassed to say that I swear like a sailor. I like the idea of being a calm grandma who can handle any situation, but that's not me.

One of the things the grandkids love to do when they come to stay is to feed the horses. It sounds idyllic. But the first time I took four of them up to the horse yards by myself, within thirty seconds, Eddy had hit Frank over the head with the aluminium feed scoop, Trixie was throwing oats around the shed and Hattie was crying because I'd yelled at her to stop doing whatever she was doing. Just as I was dragging Eddy off to the house, his father appeared, and then I got into trouble for being too emotional.

I love watching each of them growing into the person they'll be, seeing their idiosyncrasies emerge. When Eddy was tiny, he was obsessed with DVD covers. Right now, Winnie likes to carry a ball of fluff in her hand and Frank has a love affair with his soft toy, Ducky, who has been lost, run over, locked in a lunch box for six weeks and patched so many times there's scarcely a trace of the original fabric.

Eddy is always on the go. When he was two, he was dynamite. It was a battle to keep him in his sleeping bag. I used to put a safety pin on the zip to keep him in, then a twisted paperclip; I even tried a small padlock, but he could always get out. One night, something woke Will around two a.m. When he followed the noises to the kitchen, he found Eddy, who had unzipped his sleeping bag, climbed out of his cot, carried his and Frank's empty bottles to the kitchen, pulled a stool over to the fridge, climbed onto the stool, reached up and removed the 'childproof' sock that held the two fridge handles, climbed down, got the milk out and tipped it into the bottles, dragged the stool across to the microwave, climbed onto the stool again, put both bottles in the microwave and turned it on. It was the *ding* of the microwave that had woken his father.

And the kids' honesty is wonderful. At Frank's most recent

birthday, his fourth, as I handed over a parcel, Eddy muttered, 'I hope it's not stupid clothes.' When Frank peeped in and saw clothes, he dropped the parcel and moved on to the next one.

●

One of the hardest things about being a grandmother is sitting out the births, waiting to hear that everything is okay. I am like a cat on hot bricks for the last couple of weeks of the pregnancies. When I was pacing around waiting for my daughter to have her most recent baby, Will said, 'Don't worry, Mum, there's a baby born every minute. She'll be okay.' I shook my head. 'You haven't lived as long as me—you don't know how many things can go wrong.'

I knew I was going to love the grandchildren, but I didn't realise I'd fall in love with them. That's what it's like: being in love. I think about them all the time, miss them when they are away for too long and am bubbling with excitement when we are about to get together. My life has got a lot more interesting and fun. It's a deep and consuming love.

When Eddy was tiny, Will and Sam let dear friends of ours take him overnight. I hadn't even thought to offer to have him to stay—I thought he was too little to be away from his parents. So when Will casually mentioned that Eddy wouldn't be there when we called in—because he'd GONE TO STAY WITH SANDY AND PAUL!—I was inconsolable. I knew I was being a sook, but I was broken-hearted. I sobbed and sobbed. I've toughened up and am now so busy babysitting that I'm more than happy for them to go and stay with other people, but I'll never forget the immense sadness I felt then. It made me realise that if I wanted to be part of these kids' lives, I had to be involved, to offer my services and do the hard yards.

Looking back at those early days of being a new grandparent makes me smile: to see how unsure I was. Now it's nothing to have a couple of them staying the night, to change nappies, get up at all hours. Cope. But I remember looking after Eddy when he was just a little baby. I was at Will and Sam's house with their friends' ten-year-old son, Joe, who was there for the day. I think Joe had more idea about what to do than I did. 'Do you think I should pick him up?' I remember asking Joe, and being reassured by his nod.

We have terrific times together, painting, drawing, reading, building Lego, bouncing on the trampoline, playing in the cubby. When the kids come to stay, there is a circuit we do: first we go and feed the horses (there are strict rules about that now), from there we head to the swings and slide and the rings that you can hang upside down on, then to the cubby, which Sam's father built when she was a little girl; somehow it ended up at our place. There's a small kitchen with an old broken microwave and stove. One window is jammed permanently open on the side: that's where the adults stand to order pretend cappuccinos and doughnuts—we all love this game. And then to the trampoline, one of those old trampolines that are probably illegal now, a big rectangular thing with no safety net. It's on a bit of a lean downhill, so the kids' favourite game is to start uphill and *bounce, bounce, bounce* until they fly off the end of the trampoline and into my arms. Sometimes the big ones get up such momentum that they nearly knock me backwards into the Echium bush.

I'm Podge to them, not Grandma. It's the baby name that I've never shaken off and its playfulness sets the tone for the type of grandmother I am, up for anything. The kids love playing with me. I let them sit on my lap and steer as we drive around the farm, we ride the ponies, race plastic trikes down the hill to the orchard, swim, sing, tell stories and ride up the road to find tadpoles.

The times I love best are the times when there's nothing that has to be done: loafing around on Clair's bed with the knitted finger-puppets from Peru; playing 'Sharkie' in their backyard, where I'm the shark and the picnic table is the boat and you can't stay in the boat for more than thirty seconds; taking turns being the bossy teacher (Miss Cardigan) with Bear and Trix and Francesca; playing with every toy in the toy box; seeing how many different hats can be folded from a piece of silver wrapping paper.

One of the things I love about the hit series *Bluey* is how playful the family is. The adults are always happy to muck around with the kids, to delight in their wackiness. We need to remember how joyful that can be, and not get hung up on meals and chores.

Recently, I asked a friend what being a grandmother meant to her. She said it felt as though her life was complete, that she could relax, because the next generation was on its way.

I like that feeling too, that our kids are becoming the family leaders, that we are living on the edge of their lives. But what I love most is the emotional richness, the happiness these grandchildren bring to us. We are so lucky to have them.

Gillian Triggs

Grandmothers as Social Activists

Grandmothers as social activists? What a radical idea... but one that is increasingly true of today's generation of grandmothers.

A sweet memory of my time as president of the Australian Human Rights Commission was being asked by my executive assistant to look down from my Pitt Street office to the Grandmothers for Refugees singing in the street below to support the commission and its advocacy for refugees detained indefinitely in offshore detention camps. What a delight to see the men in their suits walk by in bemused wonderment. How mistaken to dismiss these grandmothers as having passed their use-by date.

Why should we be surprised? This generation of

grandmothers came from the sixties and seventies, many—and for the first time in history—spending formative years at university—with free or minimal fees—marching against Vietnam, experimenting with sexual liberation, burning our bras and 'making love not war'. Political activism is mother's milk to many of the women from those times.

Over the following years, this unique generation of women rode the crest of a wave of opportunity and optimism. The *Sex Discrimination Act (Commonwealth)* was passed in 1984... problem of equality fixed. The future was ours. And, to a significant degree, so it has been. Today, women over sixty are often well educated and financially independent, having had a fruitful career while also doing a decent job of raising their children. Today, the sixties generation of women is emerging as a political force to be reckoned with.

But wait. How can it be that the position of women in Australia has been in regression over the last fifteen years or so? Here are some disturbing facts. The fastest-growing group of homeless people in Australia is not eighteen-year-old youths sleeping under a bridge, but women over fifty-five. How ignominious and sad to have to ask your son or niece if you can sleep on their sofa for a few weeks as you can no longer pay the rent or the mortgage. Women retire today on forty-six per cent of the superannuation available to men. Why? Because we agree to accept flexible, casual and contract work with little job security or opportunities for promotion. We fall off the superannuation ladder and never catch up, despite providing most unpaid caring work across the nation.

Women are still at the bottom of the employment pyramid in female-dominated industries—as hospital paramedics and cleaners, factory workers, maids and waitresses, in hotels and restaurants and in low-paid teaching and nursing positions. The gender pay gap of around sixteen per cent is narrowing with glacial speed.

In 2006, the World Economic Forum's Gender Index placed Australia fifteenth globally, broadly among the nations we would most expect to be compared with—New Zealand, Canada, the United Kingdom, France and the Scandinavian countries. Ten years later, in 2016, we had slipped to forty-sixth. By 2018, we had gone up a few points to thirty-ninth. We remain today stubbornly consigned to the lower ranks, below Serbia, Bolivia, Laos, Latvia, Cuba and Burundi.

The WEF Global Index is measured against four indices: economic participation, health and survival, educational attainment and political empowerment. The good news is that, not surprisingly, Australian women and girls are ranked first in the world for educational attainment. But now the bad news: we are a hundred and third for health, seventy-seventh for ministerial positions in government, forty-ninth for political empowerment and forty-sixth for economic participation.

Our hopes for fair access to work were raised by Mr Abbott's promise, as leader of the opposition, of a 'rolled-gold' six months' maternity leave, only to be dashed when the political debate descended into allegations that women are 'double dippers' and 'welfare cheats'. The law for Australian women remains at eighteen weeks' paid maternity leave at minimum wage, compared with Sweden's paternity leave of 480 days at eighty per cent of salary.

How has it come to this? Why has education not ensured genuine equality? Why are Australia's women not in the streets demanding fairness from a male-dominated government and corporate sector?

Are we, at heart, just like our grandmothers? Has very little really changed? Are grandmothers, by culture or by a law of nature, destined merely to be sweet, passive, caring and kind; to stand behind their men, support the family, love their grandchildren and seek little for themselves?

My grandmother, Sarah-Jane, met all these clichéd standards. She was born in the reign of Queen Victoria, in 1899. She admirably met the traditional image of a grandmother: pretty, even in old age, white-haired and blue-eyed.

In 1958, as we stood on the deck of the *Iberia*, the flagship of the Orient and Pacific Line, leaving from Tilbury Docks for Australia, my mother said, 'Give your grandmother a special wave. She is old and we may not see her again.' Sarah-Jane was sixty-two, dressed in black, wearing pearl earrings and sixty-denier lisle stockings, wrinkled at her ankles. Widowed at fifty-three, with few financial resources—she had never been employed—Sarah-Jane was largely dependent on her daughters and sons-in-law.

She came to Melbourne several times to visit us and lived to be eighty-nine.

Sarah-Jane avoided any sort of disagreement or controversy

in private, let alone in the public arena. 'A lady's name should appear in the newspapers only three times in her life: on birth, marriage and death.' She would have been horrified to know that her granddaughter was the subject of forty-two satirical cartoons and over sixty thousand words (and counting) of newsprint castigating me for my work as president of the AHRC.

For Sarah-Jane, family was all. She believed wholeheartedly in the adage that blood is thicker than water. As one of a typically large Victorian family of eight siblings, she was never particularly interested in widening her small group of friends.

I have followed her directions for a successful dinner party. It was bad form, she believed, to engage in one-to-one private conversations; a general conversation among the group on a neutral topic was the desired objective. Sex and religion should never be discussed. In this, I have strayed from her protocol. But I also prefer a wide-ranging debate at dinner. When I was first married to my husband and joined international diplomatic life as a 'trailing spouse', I remember him accusing me of conducting seminars at official dinner parties!

Sarah-Jane might have been surprised to know that she has been a driving motivator in my life. As a teenager in the early sixties, I have a vivid memory of one of her visits, when she was sitting up in bed, counting out her small change on the bedspread to see if she could stretch her money to buy a Christmas present for each member of the family. The sum total was pitiful. Sarah-Jane had no means to increase her funds beyond whatever the family's largesse had provided her.

Mercifully, my parents were in business as jewellers and were, indeed, generous. At Christmas, we each received a modest gift from Sarah-Jane, and I treasured mine.

Yet another seemingly insignificant incident compounded my understanding of my grandmother's loss of autonomy. Like Queen Elizabeth the Queen Mother, Sarah-Jane always wore pearls: three-strand necklaces and earrings. As the earrings were clipped on (pierced ears were vulgar), she was constantly losing one. To go out in public without her pearls was unthinkable. She would ask my father, through the agency of my mother, to buy her new ones. As the saga of the lost earring was oft-repeated, my father became increasingly annoyed, but would eventually relent and provide another. I was struck at the time by the ignominy of Sarah-Jane's position. Today, if I had lost such an item, I would simply buy a replacement without a second thought. I doubt she was ever able to enjoy that freedom. Such minuscule details of ordinary life mark how things have changed for women today who have financial autonomy.

Even as a young girl, I was mortified by the evident frustration of an older woman who had so little financial independence. I vowed never to be in that position. I knew, instinctively, that to reach whatever potential one might have, it was essential, as Virginia Woolf well understood, to have 'a room of one's own'. That is not to say that money has been a catalyst for my work over the decades, but rather that a reliable income is vital to achieving autonomy.

Sarah-Jane also had a steely inner core. Arriving home

after school one day, I was shocked when she asked me, 'Will you do the ironing or shall I?' As she left the house for work that morning, my mother had apparently airily asked my grandmother to iron the ever-mounting pile of sheets, shirts and napkins, always the last household chore to be tackled. From my mother's point of view, as Sarah-Jane was at home all day, this seemed to be an entirely reasonable request. Not so for Sarah-Jane. The heat of the summer was inescapable and enervating. She was probably about seventy years old. Far better to ask a healthy teenager. I, of course, agreed to do the ironing, but filed away for future reference that my grandmother was smarter than others gave her credit for!

As Sarah-Jane sank into the oblivion of Alzheimer's, she lived out her last years in an aged-care residence in London. Whenever I returned to England, I would visit my tranquil, beautifully dressed grandmother, who, having no idea who I was, said to me, 'You're a nice young girl. Do come to see me again.' I would leave in tears, but grateful that Sarah-Jane had at least found some sort of serenity.

When delving into these sepia-tinted flashes from the past, I am surprised by how powerful—even hurtful—they remain. Why would I care today about such fleeting incidents, which one might have imagined would quickly fade? I do not know. But perhaps the psychologists would say that such early experiences shape our adult lives in profound, lasting and unexpected ways.

Sarah-Jane would not recognise my twenty-first-century role as a grandmother. At seventy-four, I am working, travelling and continuing to be outspoken. My grandchildren, Sia (aged four) and Leonard (aged two), live an international life in Paris and are becoming bilingual. I speak to them by Skype and babysit for a couple of weeks in July when the creches and schools are closed for the summer. Every second year, they come to Australia for Christmas.

I have some French and would love to speak to my grandchildren in their first language. Rightly, their parents, my son James and his French partner, Marie, insist that I speak only English, otherwise Sia and Leonard will adopt the easy option of French. Sia thinks I am intellectually rather slow. If I mispronounce a word in French or make a grammatical error (*quelle horreur*), she corrects me and, in exasperation, employs both the English and French words to ensure I get her point. I love being with such bright, energetic children and am sometimes sad that I am a distant, fly-in, fly-out spectre in their lives.

My relationship with my grandchildren will be very different from many grandparenting relationships of the past. Different but, I hope, just as special. The geographical distance means that I will not be part of the day-to-day lives of Sia and Leonard. I will not be able to pick them up from school and hear their triumphs and woes. I will always be the visitor who swans into town, breaks the household rules with forbidden treats and goes away again. I will not be there to listen to whispered hopes and fears, nor will I be a gentle, calm and constant presence in their lives.

But I will bring to Sia and Leonard that fierce loyalty for family that Sarah-Jane maintained, rightly or wrongly, as well as her warmth and integrity. I hope to be a strong influence in their lives; to stimulate, excite and support them in every way possible. Perhaps I can show them what a woman can achieve in her lifetime, given the opportunity and a dash of determination.

I suspect many women today grapple with finding a new version of the contemporary grandmother, as they retain a traditional view of a caring woman with little autonomy or life beyond her family. Grandmothers today are likely to be healthy, relatively fit and up for a game of tennis or a ski trip (on the moderate slopes). With some significant exceptions (for example, those who have no superannuation, live alone or have high medical expenses), today's grandmother will have financial means of her own, a career and a fruitful, active life. She will nurture her grandchildren, but will be less passive, more actively engaged with the world, freer to rise to her own potential and, I suggest, happier than many grandmothers in the past, with greater self-confidence.

While my generation has been uniquely privileged in so many ways, I believe that, as grandmothers, we should use our remaining years—decades—to reach out to our less privileged sisters to bring them with us. Too many women have been left behind. The promises of the sixties and seventies have not been met fully for all Australian women. We grandmothers now have a responsibility to advocate, to be politically active in using our education and financial independence to ensure equality of opportunity and outcome. For all women. How dismaying that I should have studied for a law degree, a Master of Laws and a PhD, all at the expense of the Australian, American and British taxpayers, while law students today will finish their JD degree $100,000 in debt. As grandmothers, we should be demanding affordable childcare, full superannuation even when on maternity and carers leave, equal pay for equal work, freedom from sexual harassment and bullying in employment, and protection from domestic violence at home.

As grandmothers, what do we have to lose? We are not looking for advancement in our careers. We are strong, healthy and independent. Bravo to Grandmothers for Refugees, the Older Women's Network and the scores of other women's advocacy and networking groups. Let us work together to harness the power of today's generation of grandmothers, who can and will speak up for social justice. Let us work together to achieve the vision of gender equality that we and our political leaders had in the sixties and seventies.

I like to think that, in Sarah-Jane's quiet way, she would have supported my outspokenness on human rights and forgiven me my notorious media presence. I now understand better the continuing influence she has had on my life, and thank her for it.

Postscript: I am about to leave for Geneva to take up a new role in the United Nations as Assistant High Commissioner for Protection. For the first time in my grandchildren's lives, I will be only three hours by train from Paris. It seems one should never say never. Maybe in the future I can be a more real presence in their lives than I had believed possible.

Maggie Beer

Food, Music and Soul

Being a grandmother is a gift but it's not one I've put as much time into as I'd hoped to, simply because time has ever been my enemy. But I'm working on it.

They say history repeats itself, and that's certainly true for my husband, Colin, and me. We both had parents who ran small businesses. As is the case for many who own their own businesses, we have always felt too 'outside the mould' to work for anyone else. And, as it so often happens, the work is never finished—it's the 24/7 model of life—so, although we have revelled in shaping our own destinies, I wish I could have done it better for the sake of our children.

I can't talk about my feelings as a grandmother without acknowledging this regret I live with: when our daughters, Saskia and Elli, were born, we were working so hard to survive we just didn't spend enough time with them, truly focused on them. We tried our best to make decisions that would help to compensate for the amount of time we spent working: we didn't have a television until the girls were ten and twelve years of age, respectively; we didn't open our restaurant at night; and we always ate breakfast and dinner together as a family. I do believe there is a difference between regret and guilt, and while my daughters have worked hard at releasing me from the guilt, the regret remains. I should say, however, that for all of this we managed to raise two incredibly strong, intelligent, creative and caring women.

Our wonderful daughters each have three children: my eldest grandchild, Zoe, almost twenty-three, followed closely by Max, twenty-two, Lilly, twenty, Rory, sixteen, Ben, eleven and Darby the latecomer, four years old. Each is totally different, and how wonderful that is. Despite always being time-poor, there is one thing Colin and I took to like ducks to water, and that's loving our children, and now our six grandchildren. We love them all unequivocally and will continue to forever.

When I became a grandmother, I had no family role model I wanted to follow. My mother had the most amazing spirit and zest for life and she had an older, unmarried sister, Gladys. Unmarried women were known as 'maiden aunts' within families and they often held a useful place. Aunt Gladys was very special to me. She was the person who educated me in many ways. My mother's mother died before I was born, and my father's mother kept herself withdrawn from us when we were children. Her own children, particularly my father, were important to her, but my mother was not, so there was no warmth shown to my brothers and me. Never once do I remember a kiss or a hug or any sort of affection. When we visited her, we were simply there to be seen and not heard, nor taken account of in any way.

Now that I am a grandmother, I realise more and more what complex creatures we are, and how childhood experiences have lasting impacts—children can be hurt, without even realising it at the time, by omission. I'm sure my grandmother's attitude was informed by a mixture of the mores of the time and perhaps the feeling that no one was good enough for her youngest son. But the absence of any connection with her has left a gap in the lives of her grandchildren, and I sometimes feel sad for the loss of it. My logical brain says I should leave aside the hurt caused by my grandmother's seeming indifference and accept that she has nevertheless been a big part of my life. Within the family she was a renowned cook, though more of the sweet kind. When we visited on a Sunday, we would see all manner of beautiful cakes ready for the rest of the family. They were always 'for after'. I'm absolutely certain that the cooking gene came directly from her to my father, to me and then to my oldest daughter. There has never been any doubt that the lineage began with my grandmother. For that, I am grateful to her.

My father's family were also incredibly musical; they all had such beautiful voices and a true love of music. The few times the whole family were around the piano singing,

I can only remember my grandmother sitting in a chair, not joining in. I might be doing her an injustice, but it is what I remember. My father and his brothers would sing anywhere, and the youngest girl, my auntie Gwen, sang professionally with big bands in places like Petersham Town Hall. I heard her sing just once; I was ten and allowed to sneak upstairs to listen. I will never forget the atmosphere and the sultry sound of her voice. This love of music is so much a part of me, and now of my grandchildren too, that I have to acknowledge its source in my grandmother and her family.

When our first grandchild was born nearly twenty-three years ago, I was both full of apprehension—was I really ready to be a grandmother?—and determined that things would be different from my own experience with my grandmother. I'll never forget the joy of each grandchild's birth and the emotional bonds we forged with them, which still remain today.

I really did want to be different with my grandchildren: this was my chance not only to be a better grandmother than mine had been to me, but also to be a better grandmother than I had been as a mother. I believe this sentiment guides many of us from one generation to the next. I am thankful that in some ways I've succeeded in being marginally better as a grandmother than as a mother. While I'm just as busy, I think I really have taken the chance to foster the individual spark in each child. There is such joy in that.

Not for a moment, though, is it plain sailing. My grandchildren are growing up in a much more difficult world than we did, or even than our children, their parents, did, and at times it distresses me. I certainly worry for them. I can't always understand the complexities of their issues, nor can I always help guide them to solutions, but I hope that their knowing we love them unconditionally will go some way to helping them in their lives.

My mother was a person who, no matter how hard things were, found such joy in life, and every time I glimpsed the kind, smiling face of her mother in photographs, I knew I had missed out on someone important in my life. Some ten years ago, I met a man who had been my mother's boyfriend when she was in her late teens. He had been part of not only Mum's life at that time, but also that of her parents and her brothers. That meeting gave me such happiness because, even at his age, over ninety, he could recall spending time at my mother's home: he told me how he had played bridge with my grandmother, and how warm and generous she was, and how there were always young people coming and going in the house. She never lived to know her grandchildren. How I would love to have known her.

Life was different for us as a family with the first four of our grandchildren. Our way of being with them then was to gather, always on a Sunday afternoon, for what the family still calls 'late lunch/early dinner'. By eating at four p.m. the littlest child didn't become overtired and cranky and the cousins could enjoy playing around our dam in the 'bamboos of doom', as they called them, or playing cricket, or swimming in the pool, while we ate outside—under the huge wisteria if it was summer, or by a firebox if it was winter. Our favourite time as a family is still Sunday afternoon, sharing a meal. Almost without exception it is eating outside in the courtyard, even in winter. All our family celebrations are around a meal.

When Zoe was about four she said to me: 'Nonna, can I have a proper job? Not just plucking parsley!' When Lilly was about seven, she came with me to a cooking class on the banks of the river in Adelaide. It was a class for children aged seven to ten and Lilly really wanted to be the one to show them what to do. This caused some mirth among the families watching on. After it was over, a journalist interviewed Lilly and asked when she'd started cooking. I'll never forget her pausing, then saying: 'All my life, really.' It is true. Lilly loved to cook from an early age: when we all came together for a meal, Lilly would have baked bread or been the one to make the birthday cake. Lilly was often like a mother hen to her siblings and could produce a meal in the blink of an eye. I love that at nineteen she took herself off to Europe on a working holiday and straight into a job at the Dorchester. This love of food, the work ethic she gained as a child, helping her mum cook and sell food at the Barossa Markets, getting up at five a.m. on weekends as a teenager, all stood her in good stead for her future.

Our daughters have, in their own ways, followed our footsteps into the commercial food world, and they too came to a stage in their growing businesses where they worked every weekend, just as we had when they were children. So, while our Sunday meals can't happen as often now, we are still in their lives every day in some small way, and every family occasion is celebrated by sharing beautiful food around the table. I might never have been the grandmother who babysat at the drop of a hat, but I would roll pasta with them when they were young, or have them help me pick herbs from the garden, or read poetry to them while they cuddled into me, waiting for their parents to collect them.

Together, Colin and I have had a part in developing in each grandchild something very individual. With Zoe the love of reading and poetry defines her in many ways, but she also loves music. We took Zoe and Max to their first opera when they were young. They absorbed it like sponges and now Zoe takes herself and doesn't mind going alone. Max is and always has been artistic. At primary school, when there were no 'rules' about art, his large works were breathtaking. When the right time comes he'll pick up art again but music is his fundamental love. Classical music was always a natural part of my daily life when I was growing up and Max is the same. I always loved it when Max would be listening to 'his music' on headphones and pass them over to me to listen, saying: 'Nonna, you'll love this one.' And he was always right. It is a strong link between us.

Sixteen-year-old Rory, the enigma, the thinker of big thoughts, with the humour of a stand-up comedian, is also creative, always drawing or painting, but doesn't like to be defined by that. I was so chuffed when, just recently, knowing it was something I so want to do, he suggested we could enrol in a sculpture course together.

Ben, twelve, is the sportsman of the family, following his

grandad and mum's sporting prowess—and totally unlike his nonna, I have to say. Earlier this year, I gained so many brownie points when I was invited to a Port Power football game by the chairman of the board, Kochie, and took Ben along. I enjoyed a beautiful lunch, the best seats in the house at an action-packed game, and I had Ben next to me, explaining the intricacies of the game. I don't get to watch Ben play sport as often as I would like, but I love that he will run up to me and give me a big hug in front of his mates without any embarrassment. None of the grandchildren has ever been embarrassed by public displays of affection.

Darby, the youngest, now four, is full of life and so cheeky. Her love of music is innate: as soon as she hears it, she moves to the beat. Somehow, being the youngest, she can also hold court. When all the grandchildren are around the table, the eldest having cooked the dinner, their parents not in sight, Darby makes sure she has her say, whichever way the conversation is going.

How lucky I am that we live in the Barossa, that we farm for ourselves and can be part of looking after our own environment. By having a country lifestyle, my grandchildren are closer to the earth, closer to the source of our food, and have an understanding of the importance of looking after the land. Yes, they do worry about the future. Yet I see in the young such passionate advocates of change and I know they will do everything in their power to be part of the awareness and action for a sustainable future. I have faith that we are in good hands.

I remain 'Nonna' to all my grandchildren, not because of any Italian heritage, but because of a love of the Italian sensibility and the softness of the sound of 'Nonna', rather than the harsher-sounding 'Grandma' we used in my childhood. My life, our family's lives, are so much richer thanks to our grandchildren. I am a hugely lucky person and an even luckier Nonna.

Ramona Koval

For What Has Been and What Will Be

A woman holding a scalpel dives into the wine-dark waters off the Sardinian Island of Sant'Antioco. She swims to the secluded seagrass beds, home of the endangered Mediterranean clam, *Pinna nobilis*. Here, early in the morning, by the light of the late spring's full moon, she collects the *byssus* or sea silk produced by the clam's *byssus* gland—keratin threads that anchor the shell to the rocks.

At this time of year, the mud of the lagoon is soft; she can extract the animal, cut the *byssus* filaments and replace the clam without damaging it, thus abiding by the rules of the European Union Habitats Directive.

After one hundred dives, she has gathered only thirty grams of *byssus*. Back in her studio, she removes the sea sediment with a carding comb and rinses the fibres in fresh water. Then she spins them into silky thread finer than that of silkworms, a third the width of a human hair, chanting melodies taught to her by her grandmother, intoning prayers in a mixture of Sardo (the ancient Sardinian dialect) and Hebrew. She prays *for what has been and what will be*. Watching her on my computer screen, I recognise the Hebrew words *Elohim* and *Adonai*, two of the names given to the God of Moses. She dyes the strands in secret concoctions of lemon juice, spices and varieties of seaweed. The fibres soon become elastic and shimmer in the sunlight like threads of gold.

The ancient Egyptians, Greeks, Romans and Chinese all make mention of sea silk, sometimes calling it sea wool, or mermaid silk. In Jules Verne's *Twenty Thousand Leagues Under the Sea*, the crew of the *Nautilus* wore clothes of spun sea silk.

Now in her sixties, Chiara Vigo claims she is the last woman alive who knows the secrets of working *byssus*, secrets that are whispered, never written, entrusted from woman to woman, the daughters and granddaughters in her family, for twenty-four generations. She remembers her grandmother teaching her, aged three, to dive. Her surname reveals her family to be from Spain or Liguria. Local Sardinians were not sailors but shepherds, afraid of the sea, which for them was the portal for invasions from abroad—Phoenicians, Arabs and Catalans. Many had never seen the sea, much less learned to swim.

According to the *Sea Oath* she is bound by, the precious *byssus*, like the sun, or the tides, or the flight of an eagle, can never be bought or sold. There is a sign on the door of her studio, the *Museo del Bisso*: *Haste doesn't live here.*

Vigo embroiders the *byssus* thread onto pieces of fabric, or braids bracelets as gifts or for those who seek her help: *byssus* is said to bring both good fortune and fertility. Her work is displayed in the Louvre, the Vatican and the British Museum.

By twelve Vigo knew how to weave, but who will collect and spin the fine silk when she is gone? Her daughter lives in Dublin, and in 2017 told the BBC: 'My mother and I are very different. People have always told me that I'd be a fool to allow this art to die, but I'm desperately torn. My life is mine.'

Might there be no more mermaid silk for the coming generations? We have our own miraculous man-made fibres now, and cheaper and more efficient ways to manufacture threads that look golden, so why does it seem such a pity to allow the hidden knowledge of *byssus*—the word itself sounds like a whispered prayer—to fade and die?

•

How I longed to be a granddaughter in a long line of grand-daughters, like Chiara Vigo, learning secret chants from my grandmother and, when the day came, teaching them to my own grandchildren. But fate had delivered me to a mother who was a Holocaust survivor, the only one out of her once large Polish Jewish family. Here was I at the bottom of the world, a child with no grandparents. At special school assemblies, when grandparents filled the rows, I sang for nobody. Old people remained a mystery.

At fifty-one I became a grandmother to Maya. With no fond memories of being grandmothered, I was free to create my own role. But who I should be? Certainly not a silly old woman fooled by the wolf in *Little Red Riding Hood*?

Over the next nine years my brood enlarged—Maya was joined two years later by her sister Eden, and a few months after that their cousin Bella arrived. Nearly three years passed and then we welcomed the twins, Milly and Jesse, a girl and our only boy, and finally, four years after that, Layla completed the picture.

I taught my grandchildren to call me *Booba*, Yiddish for grandmother, a word linguistically related to the Slavic *Baba*, and through this to the story of *Baba Yaga*, the mythic Grandmother Witch. She lived in a cottage built upon outsized chicken's feet and surrounded by a fence made from human bones, the results of her penchant for cooking and eating people who displeased her. But some stories tell of her offering guidance to those who approached her with open- ness and honesty. Connected to the supernatural power of the underworld, she was eternally wise, knowing the medicinal secrets of plants and potions and flying in a magic mortar, the pestle a rudder.

Could I have the courage and wisdom of *Baba Yaga* without her ghoulish streak? I knew I could defend my grand- children against schoolyard bullies and unreasonable teachers and adult predators. I could provide my home, a place where they would always be safe and welcome, with clean, comfort- able beds and delicious food. I would be a wise truth-teller of my own making, explaining the world with frankness and humour. I would read them stories and do all the voices. There would be unlimited kisses.

.

I am a swot by nature, so my disconnection from the line of grandmothers that had preceded me fostered a dispassionate examination of grandmothering. I even extended my research to other mammals. Like grandmother killer whales, human grandmothers live many years beyond the end of their fertility—thanks to menopause. Our fellow primates— chimps, for example—die soon after their fertility ends. So this gift of extra years must have an evolutionary value.

Killer whale grandmothers live for twenty-five years after menopause, long enough to see the oldest of their grand-calves to sexual maturity. There is much variation in foraging tactics between killer whale kin groups. Some learn to take fish from fishing trawlers, others know the timing and location for catching particular salmon species. This cultural knowledge is taught by the wise elders.

Unlike many of our fellow land mammals, human babies are born unable to stand, much less walk or find food. In the wild, parents, especially mothers, must feed them, protect them, keep them at the right temperature, avoid them becoming some predator's lunch, wash them, not drop them, not crush them while sleeping, not let them be attacked by siblings, and not strangle them out of stress and sleep-deprivation. We are immensely social creatures, and human societies have put sanctions in place to prevent such transgressions, and much attention is required for their coordination.

When I held my own baby for the first time, I was overcome with the crushing weight of responsibility to keep the child alive, breathing and whole. In the first two months of her life, I dreamed that my baby's head fell off onto the floor, and that I made a shameful attempt to secure the head back on the neck with sticky-tape. When I began helping to care for my infant grandchildren, the effort, time, attention and sheer complexity of it seemed a revelation from the wiser perspective of grandmotherhood. I see parents at their wits' end, wheeling prams erratically in the street, their splotchy, red-eyed toddlers having nonetheless survived their infancy. Someone, perhaps the grandmother, has helped shepherd the infants through vulnerable times.

I noticed more and more grandmothers at kindergarten and school pickup times. If you couldn't discern them by their clothes and laugh lines, the grandmothers were obvious as the ones holding surprises of unsuitable afternoon tea, chocolates and sweet biscuits, while the mothers picking up their own children cast disapproving glances.

A study of modern Hadza hunter-gatherers in Tanzania found grandmothers were more important to child survival than fathers, who went out every day to feed themselves and hunt, but who were successful in bringing home nutritious meat only 3.4 per cent of the time. Women, young and old, were providing the majority of calories for the women and children of the family. The old women, for example, were digging deep in the ground for calorie-rich tubers. Humans resume ovulation quickly after giving birth, which means a Hadza mother might have a helpless infant, a two-year-old, a five-year-old and a seven-year-old, all of whom have to be fed—a task only possible with the help of the still-fit grandmothers.

I once went honey-ant collecting with a group of Pitjantjatjara grandmothers in Central Australia. They spent hours in the sun digging a hole deep enough to crouch in and then extracted less than a mug-full of ants, whose abdomens were distended with golden honey. Back at camp, when the children were given this treasure, they bit off the abdomens to release the sweet nectar into their mouths.

In most tribal human societies, old people are esteemed, not because of any formal status, but because the younger people have an innate respect and admiration for them. The elderly have knowledge of important matters: folklore, magic, hunting, rituals, decision-making and medicine. There is a touch of *Baba Yaga* to this. But this status does not always last their whole lifetime. In some societies, once old people lose their mental faculties, they are considered incompetent. Some are even killed, or at least abandoned to their deaths.

Now that my direct responsibilities for children are not so urgent, I can afford to take the longer view. In the face of my looming irrelevance, I feel an urgent need to tell my children and grandchildren what I know about the world, what I have learned through struggle and failure. Am I naive in thinking they might avoid the worst and find the best if they are armed with my lessons?

Many Neanderthal women were probably grandmothers by the time they were thirty. Their grandchildren also had a prolonged childhood, and the evidence from their bones and teeth indicates it may have even been slightly longer than ours. For hundreds of thousands of years, each Neanderthal generation led the same kind of lives as the last one, and grandmothers' tales must have been important for transmitting traditions, assuming they had the ability to speak. But what could they have possibly told their little ones about the advent of the fearsome strangers, *Homo sapiens*, striding across their hills and valleys with their odd-shaped heads and their newfangled throwing spears and their obedient hunting-dog companions? They could not have known what was in store for their grandchildren: that in a thousand years or so their species would be extinct.

•

At the Japanese takeaway, I ask if there is a carry bag. Told of the charge, I grimace and pack my arms with the items. 'Booba, it's okay,' says my eldest granddaughter, attuned to my sighs. 'It's a good thing they're charging for plastic bags. They're not good for the environment.' 'I know, I know,' I tell her.

I *do* know. It's a small thing, but it is a significant change when you have been used to certain conveniences. I think of my assumptions that the tap will deliver water when I turn it, that there will be power when I press the light switch. The rise in average global temperature has already been 1.8 degrees

Celsius just in my lifetime. I read graphs and measurements and watch the news about rising carbon dioxide levels with unease.

The rate of warming increased steeply in the mid-1970s, when my children were born, and each of the last three decades has been warmer than all the decades before that since 1850. The Bureau of Meteorology projects that, without emissions control, by 2090 my city, Melbourne, will be ten per cent drier and 3.8 degrees Celsius hotter than now. Fifty-degree days could occur by the 2040s; in those temperatures, hospitals, electricity systems and infrastructure would all struggle. Already the bitumen on the roads softens in the heat. What can I tell my grandchildren about what they might expect? *Haste doesn't live here* might be the watchword on Chiara Vigo's studio, but not for me. Time is running out and I have no time to lose. Like Chiara Vigo, I am already in my sixties and, while I will avoid the worst consequences of climate change, I fear that my grandchildren won't.

Some have farsighted plans to escape to an alternative planet once ours becomes unfit for life. Even if I was younger and single, I doubt I would sign up for the training and the Martian voyage and then settle on a cold planet covered with deserts, subject to dust storms that can last for months, and with a thin atmosphere made up mostly of carbon dioxide, which we can't breathe. I dislike the idea of being stuck on a cruise ship, much less a never-ending cruise ship of testy Martian pioneers, without a buffet service. But I am a curious creature, so I am nevertheless fascinated by the stories we tell ourselves about what it might be like to be on one of those voyages: I imagine having my heart in my mouth as we deal with the small and large threats and victories en route.

But while we watch movies and dream about fantastic voyages, we hear news of floods and droughts and wildfires and hurricanes. I think of the people close to those disasters and thank my lucky stars that I am not them. But we are all them, or might be very soon.

We are different from Neanderthal grandmothers in that we do know what's in store. One of our most powerful fore-casting tools is a deep understanding of our history and how to use it to chart new courses. What help to our grandchildren is the sentimental mystery of *byssus* and other ancient songs? Chiara Vigo prays *for what has been and what will be*. Prayer? We need to do more than pray. We can tell our stories of what will be with so much more data now, and we can encourage and model urgent action beyond the whispered secrets and the confines of the hearth and home.

And anyway, is Chiara Vigo really the last woman alive who holds the secret of *byssus*? A deeper investigation into the mysteries of Sant'Antioco reveals a rival sea silk collective: the sisters Assuntina and Giuseppina Pes learned the secrets from Efisia Murroni, who herself was instructed by Italo Diana at a school for weaving that opened on the island in 1923. In 2013, the Pes sisters ran a *byssus* workshop and explained every step of the process to the participants. There were no chants, prom-ises and obligations here, but there was documentation, which was presented to a conference organised in the Italian town of

Lecce by the Centre for Textile Research at the University of Copenhagen.

In 2016, the local municipality closed Chiara Vigo's *Museo del Bisso* because of noncompliant electrical installations. She claims they were forcing her to charge entrance fees and 'to write down my secrets'. She says she now wants to live overseas.

I am a little sorry to ruin a perfectly enchanting story. We are readily seduced by the hushed prayers, the diving by moonlight, the golden threads, but now, more than anything, we need to convey to our grandchildren our lived wisdom, together with our data and our fighting spirit. Defending these children should now reach well beyond the schoolyard, outwards towards a global movement for action and change, as we take flight in our magic mortars, wielding our pestles as rudders.

We are all *Baba Yaga* now.

Yvette Holt

G'andma

Dedicated to my Mother –
Marlene Rosalie Clarice Holt (née Henry)
8/08/1945 – 22/07/2019

The grandfather clock on the wall promises me that it is 2:40 p.m. (Australian Central Standard Time). In ten to fifteen minutes or so my grannies will be bowling through the double front gates of our home out here in Larapinta, a western outskirts suburb of Alice Springs stencilled in the colours of ancient sienna and terracotta canvas. School ports will be abandoned somewhere along the lawn-less pebbly path between the driveway and front porch. I will juggle their ports with open arms before our family dog Kele (pronounced colour)—half-bullmastiff, half-dingo—decides to do some collecting of her own, using those elongated toothy-pegs. Larapinta lies between the world-famous Larapinta Trails and the pristine cradling caterpillar-like mountains of the glorious Yeperenye (MacDonnell Ranges). From our home, you could throw a frisbee to trails that lead you to the historic Telegraph Station north-east, Desert Park south-west, Simpsons Gap to the west, or Mount Gillen directly adjacent to Larapinta.

Transitioning from a mother to a grandmother left very few margins distinguishing the two chapters; I was twenty-four when I had my only child, my daughter, Cheyenne, and then by the age of thirty-nine I had become a grandmother. Suddenly, astonishingly, and surprisingly to all who knew me, I had been inducted into the Grandmother Hall of Fame. As course coordinator, lecturer and researcher in the fields of Creative Writing, Aboriginal Women's Studies, and Australian Indigenous Studies, I went from organising the babysitter to *being the babysitter.* I will leave you to do the maths.

Writing about our roles as grandmothers is deeply anchored in both what has preceded and what has succeeded our roles as mothers—this is truth-telling at its finest. As a First Nation Aboriginal grandmother, I would also like to think that my intergenerational memory of landscape, while it does not conform me, does, however, inform me.

Albert Einstein once said, 'You don't really understand something unless you can explain it to your grandmother.' I relate to this, particularly because of the immersive relationship that I hold so dearly with my own trio of grandchildren. Over time I have learnt that being a grandmother is one thing.

Becoming a grandmother is entirely different.

When I am home in Alice Springs, around two p.m., I wrap everything up in my makeshift writing studio—that is, the kitchen dining table. Paperwork stacked away, laptop, tablet, books, journals, sticky notes, editorials, pens and highlighters all magically vanish into G'andma's secret closet. Wrapping things up means responding to a freight train of emails, winding up telephone conferences, gathering the washing, folding uniforms, clearing the dish stack, vacuuming, ensuring beds are made, emptying the trash, emptying the mailbox and emptying my psyche for a clean slate of grandchildren afternoon delight. There, now I am prepared for the flowing indoor foot-stomps of my little people and their excitable rising voices. This routine is not sometimes; it is not every now and then; it is not maybe it will happen, maybe it won't—when I am home it happens daily.

Journal Entry: May, 2019, 6:38 a.m. I woke up this morning cursing my iPhone for not being fully charged. Today of all days I slept in. Bugger! Duvet thrown off like a wretched sixteenth-century heretic curse. Making a marathon run into the bathroom, brushing my teeth, I look around from tap to tile for three more toothbrushes. Then I realised I was no longer in Larapinta but in my dear friend's home, in Brunswick, Melbourne. Such is the endearing emotional and psychological template of grandmotherhood that, whenever I go away, wherever I may hang my beret, I am still involved with the daily activities of my grandchildren. I miss them dreadfully. Especially first thing in the morning. I have been in Melbourne now for almost a whole month. No matter how incidental a toothbrush may seem, in my chaotic world of check-ins and departures, the 'toothbrush' is more than just symbolic; it is a statement that says 'G'andma is here with us'!

As noted by the clock on the wall, Bailey, Harper-Yvette and Arnica are arriving home from school fashionably on time. The school shirts have fluttered out of their waists, their hair shows no signs of being pinned seven hours earlier by a layering of *don't move me unless you can smooth me* gel. The art work of stick figures and finger paintings that they're waving in the air will be magnetised onto whatever side of the refrigerator or freezer chest remains unclaimed. I have within my grasp a Picasso, a Van Gogh and a Namatjira. That is why G'andma is the writer of the family and not the painter.

After-school home-time usually signals one of two pressing matters which will swiftly need addressing before their mother arrives home from work: either their tummies will churn for an afternoon school snack (the kind their mother would frown upon) or they are bored before they have even clapped eyes on the treats I have hidden for them under their pillows. Interestingly enough, all electronic mobile devices, excluding the remote for the television, will now be on a mission to seek and enjoy. Well, that is at least until their mother gets home, and then from that time all handheld devices will return to the hide-and-seek domain of the linen cupboard. If grandmotherhood carries any authority for surpassing motherhood, I can concur that if mother says 'no', ask G'andma. The answer will usually be a resounding *yes*!

The first rule of home-time, before anyone is allowed to enter the kitchen, is to scrub your hands clean all the way up to the elbows and then go into the bedrooms and change into your yard clothes (as my mother used to call them). I whisk through the hallway picking up the deposits of navy-blue school socks strewn halfway down the corridor like a sandpit runway. Nobody cares to watch the Smart TV anymore—I look at it sitting up all alone in the living room like a dark submarine caisson ready to submerge into the void. Since when did afternoon television become so passé among Generation Z?

G'andma did you charge my phone? G'andma I can't find my Ipad—can you help me pleeeeeease? Smart TV—not so smart anymore!

Before I introduce you to my grandchildren, it would be almost entirely remiss of me not to present my mother, the woman who provided me with lifelong examples of words and actions enveloped in wisdom, thus forming my foundation of protection, nurture and above all unconditional love. My mother, a most beloved wife, a loving and most cherished mum, grandmother and great-grandmother. Mum knew an encyclopaedic thing or two about motherhood and grand-motherhood and great-grandmotherhood.

Mum was raised by her paternal Aboriginal-Afghan grandmother (Cecelia Henry, 1891–1962, Taroom Lower Dawson River, Yiman Nation Queensland) on Woorabinda

Settlement in the 1950s and 1960s. Mum's mum (Agnes Henry, 1917–1949 (née Thomas) Chillagoe, Wakaman Nation, Queensland) died suddenly from a mysterious illness—ovarian cancer was presumed.

The dilemma was this: my mum, along with her two younger sisters, Rosina (two), Jemima (six months) – three sisters born of the same mother and father could equate to being sent off to three separate missions throughout the state of Queensland, never to be in contact or know of each other again. This was oh-so-easily achievable with a quick name change at the stroke of a missionary's pen. Mum's father (Marshall Henry, 1904–1976, Taroom, Lower Dawson River, Yiman Nation Queensland), a well-known cattle stockman, needed to travel wherever the work called in order for him to provide for his family. Rather than orphan out the three girls, Mum's grandmother approached the government authorities of that time (under the *Aboriginal Protection and Restrictions of the Sale of Opium Act 1897 Queensland*), stating that she would be best suited as the sole caregiver for her three granddaughters.

The relationship that developed between my mother and her grandmother is something I had only dreamed of reading in fairytales. Instead of *Little Red Riding Hood* or *There Was an Old Woman Who Lived in a Shoe*, my childhood picture book would be illustrated with members of my own family from start to finish. The loyalty, the devotion, the admiration my mother and her grandmother held for each other was consecrated within its own cultural framework and language, heralding from the Yiman Nation. Regardless of your ethnic or cultural background, there just do not seem to be enough stories or verse memoirs written about intergenerational matrilineal relationships, stories that should pass on from one grandmother to another. I am most fortunate that my great-grandmother left such an indelible impression on my mother that it has carried into the generations who have succeeded her. An infinite source of survival and love.

I would not be the woman I am today had it not been for the indomitable matriarchal lineage that runs broadly through my veins. And even though I did not meet my great-grandmother, Cecelia (Sissy) Henry, still I miss her. Still I whisper her name to the towering ghost gums scattered along the dry riverbeds and walkways of Alice Springs. I imagine her and my mother sitting atop the branches, the dry winds flowing through their stories, and even though I am living more than some 2060 kilometres from home, I am reminded of this saying by Chief Seattle: 'There is no death. Only a change of worlds.' I thank my great-grandmother for responding to the call to raise my mother and her two younger sisters as her own children in an era when it would have been much easier to remain undetected under the prying government eyes of the Australian Assimilation Policy (1951–1962), if you were clever enough to succeed—and my great-grandmother was *clever*.

Journal Entry: August, 2019: 4:30 a.m. I am vigorously running my thumb through cartons of moleskin journals of last year and last decade to extract memories of birthing, birthdays, tooth-fairy

itineraries, potty-training, first days of school, family anecdotes
and endless scribbles of Peppa Pig (oink, oink) to name a few
snippets. I tell you truthfully, I want to write for this anthology,
Grandmothers, *but in all sincerity, I have no idea where to*
begin. My tummy has been somersaulting over what the other
cohort of Australian grandmothers must be writing about. I don't
possess a green thumb—gardens are for succulents competing with
the weeds. I don't bake blueberry muffins or apple pie—that's
what the microwave is for. And the only thing I can sew is a suite
of poems ready to hit 'send' for submission. Okay, just breathe,
Yvette, just breathe, take it one day at a time. Just string your
memories of childhood and motherhood together and then plough
into grandmotherhood. You can do this, you know you can. I
believe in you!

My grannies.

Kevin Bailey Holt (b. November 2010)—out of the three
grandchildren, his was the birth I was present for. I was more
than present for his impending birth; I sang Bailey out of his
young mother's womb with tears of fear, heartache, joy and
a love that flowed through every fibre of my being. I birthed
him through songlines of spirit from journey to arrival. In
the private birthing suite of the Mater Misercordiae Mothers'
Hospital, Brisbane, I drew on a strength within my core that
I never knew existed. It was a moment of empowerment
through matriarchal forces. Those songlines continue.

Many times, throughout the labour of Bailey, I thought
I would pass out from fear of the unknown. I held my

daughter's hand through her every breath. When the midwife said, 'Congratulations. Here you are, Grandma—a beautiful, healthy baby boy,' I was speechless. A nurse then handed me the steel surgical scissors so I could cut the umbilical cord. I looked at this rope of life entwining my child and my grandchild and was overcome with seasons of mixed emotions. I burst into tears and cried.

To this day, my eyes fill with tears when I think about how blessed I was to be there to welcome my grandson into this universe. I counted ten little fingers, ten tiny toes and marvelled at the knitting frown, which funnily enough resembles my Dad's furrows. For seven of the nine months my daughter carried my first grandchild, she slept by my side every night. Every night, I felt this little being growing inside my daughter's body. On the night of Bailey's arrival, I went home, exhaled, and walked into our kitchen; the first thing I saw was a Frida Kahlo fridge magnet, with the words: *At the end of the day, we can endure so much more than we think we can.* Truth!

My Bailey, a voracious bookworm, a backyard golfing caddy to his Poppy, an explorer of science, maths and Australian history. Bailey is the quietly spoken, gentle boy who feels deeply about the world around him. I am called G'andma by my grandchildren because Bailey could not curl his toddler tongue around the 'r' in grandma—and so G'andma I am.

Harper-Yvette Holt (b. October 2012)—my first-born granddaughter, the butterfly whisperer. Harps is one of the most astute, caring and sensitive six-year-old girls you could ever hope to meet. She is the nurturer of her little nestling family. Out of the three grandchildren, Miss Harper walks in the footprints of my mother even more so than my daughter and I do. Family albums of my childhood are her private windows into the world she says surrounds her playtime. Inquisitive beyond belief, Harps will question every corner of every page in my album of memories. She is the deep thinker and storyteller of our family. Protective of her older brother and younger sister, Harps will hold you when you cry, tickle you when you laugh and love you back tenfold when you hug her. When Harper was four years old, she would insist that I grab a chair, that we sit in the backyard with our eyes shut, in total silence. I would ask: 'Why do I have to be silent? Why can't I move? Why do I have to shut my eyes?' Harps would respond: 'Because the butterflies will come to us if we're sitting still, and then they'll sit on our hands and play with our fingers. No peeking out of your eyes, G'andma. Butterflies don't have ears, they listen with their wings, so you can't move 'cause that will scare them, and they don't like people staring at them, so eyes shut, please. Don't you know anything, G'andma? I thought you were s'posed to know everything, G'andma?' Apparently not. Mischievous, adventurous, fun-loving and a fabulous little chef to boot, Harper is a second daughter to her G'andma. Faces, hair, one's stride, the colouring of one's skin may differ from one generation to the next, but memories remain. Harper-Yvette, an old soul living in a young body.

Arnica Scout Holt Appo (b. February 2016)—the baby of

the family. Out of my three grandchildren, Arnica is more like the actual granny, the little granddaughter; whereas Bailey and Harper, I feel, are an extension of my motherhood. Arnica, with her shock of dark, thick, curly hair, throws back to my mother. Arnica, the glamour princess who loves to play with dress-ups, can turn from an Elsa to a Moana in minutes, even with a loungeroom wardrobe malfunction. Arnica is a walker and talker just like her G'andma; she sits at the helm of the dining table with gusto and manners and loves to tell her brother and sister what to eat first and when they may leave the table. A keen astronomer, nail beautician, bathroom mermaid and architect of doll-houses made solely from paddle-pop sticks, Arnica is also the logical thinker, the gracious peacemaker of our family. We await to see her personality and dreams blossom before us.

Am I not triply blessed to have two granddaughters and a grandson to comb my hair, to scratch my back, to trace their handprints inside my favourite poetry books with permanent markers (*aaargh*), to lounge across my lap at storytime? Giggling our way through almost an entire packet of arrowroot biscuits, dunking into our teacups—I feel as if I am the grandmother who refuses to age in the company of greatness.

Journal Entry: June, 2019, 10:37 p.m. Today was a good day with my psychoanalyst. I told her that I rode my pushbike all the way from Alice Springs to Fitzroy North and on the way I stopped at Oodnadatta to pick scrambled eggs out of my hair—Arnica had fed them to me the morning before, so I would not go hungry along the way. She rubbed the breakfast delight all over my head and said: 'G'andma, you have mouths all over your brains, here is more eggs for you to eat on your bike.' *As soon as I arrived in Melbourne, I changed from my designer R.M. Williams, belt-buckled corduroy shorts and fishnet stockings into a pair of sunflower aquatic coveralls that someone had packed with a little note that read:* 'just in case it rains in norf fishroy. Your legs are very muscly G'andma, you don't want to ruin your legs with a lot of water.' *Signed Harper.*

I am sitting lightning-bolt-upright in 'the chair', going one-on-one with my analyst, the relief in the air is palpable; Bailey whispers into my ear: 'G'andma, when you are finished with Melbourne, don't forget to come home. If your bike is too tired to ride, I will save up for a new one when I am twenty. We love you. PS could you please buy me a new toothbrush?'

and so, the stories
    the memories
        the dream-cycles
    the laughter
        the language
        and the love continues to grow

        flowing from one generation to the next

        truly, I am blessed

        past, present and future

Judith Brett

My Grandmother's House

I became a grandmother last year, at sixty-nine, to a lively girl born to my youngest daughter. My grandmother was forty-eight when I was born and when she died I was thirty-seven, pregnant with my granddaughter's mother. People say that seventy is the new fifty, but it's not true. My grandmother had held the hands of my first two children. I doubt I'll do the same for little Helena. There is a relentless logic to generational succession.

A grandmother for barely a year, I have thought a lot about the gifts I might bestow on the newest member of our family. Inevitably, perhaps, these are the gifts my grandmother gave me: love and a visceral sense of the past.

My grandmother lived on a farm in the Goulbourn Valley, where she kept chooks, helped with the milking and cooked on a woodstove for my grandfather and uncles. Twice a year, our family spent a week at the farm. She was my father's mother, and my brother, sister and I adored her, as did our cousins. And we all loved the farm, which seemed to exist in its own self-contained world, barely connected to the bureaucratic rhythms of schools and trains that governed our house in the suburbs.

The past was everywhere: iron bedsteads, old farm machinery, a tumble-down blacksmith's shed with a huge pair of bellows, my grandparents' wedding portraits, my father's old schoolbooks, a cable tram from the North Carlton line converted into a sleep-out, my grandfather's rambling anecdotes about his exploits as a water diviner, my grandmother's more contained stories of my father as a child and her short time as a teacher at Cummeragunga, an Aboriginal settlement on the Murray, before she married. There were remnant middens too, where patches of charcoal and broken mussel shells interrupted the furrows, and a canoe tree standing on the edge of what was once a swamp. With little sense then of the horror of Indigenous dispossession, to us this tree was just one of the things that made us feel like special children. I pitied my friends whose grandparents lived in neat Californian bungalows on quiet suburban streets, even if their grandmothers were better cooks than mine.

The first of my grandmother's gifts was unconditional love. My parents loved me unconditionally too, but they also had to bring me up and rein me in, and I had to find out how I was not them. Some ambivalence is necessary in our feelings for our parents, but there's no need for it with a grandmother who makes no demands and is interested in everything you do. This is the ideal grandmother, the one celebrated in the many sentimental grandmother quotes on the internet, who 'remembers all of your accomplishments and forgets all of your mistakes'. Of course, many grandmothers are not like this at all, but I was lucky. Once I was old enough to travel alone, I would take the train up in my school and university holidays and stay for a week. I would read, walk, daydream and have my grandmother all to myself, chatting away with her about my life and hers.

When I read Gaston Bachelard's *The Poetics of Space* in my twenties, I knew what he was talking about: the house as a cosmos, holder of memories, shelter for dreams, securing me in the world. But it was not Bachelard's storied European house of cellars, front parlours and attics that was lodged in my unconscious. It was my grandmother's single-storey wooden farmhouse with a corridor down the middle, a big kitchen, lots of doors opening to wide verandahs and the shimmering light of a flood plain. Bachelard imagines the house as vertical; mine is horizontal, and I much prefer plains to mountains or even rolling hills. But, like him, I imagine the house as safe, where I am who I am.

I know not all houses are safe, that dangers can lurk, like the evil fairies in the Grimms' fairy tales, waiting to curse unsuspecting young girls, that houses can hide the sexual and emotional abuse of women and children, and sometimes of men too. But I never lived in such a house. Coming back from a walk at nightfall, I would see my mother and grandmother through the lighted kitchen window, preparing our tea, and feel happy. Gothic tales of haunted houses, the sharp-edged empty suburbia of John Brack's paintings, Howard Arkley's blank windows, even Elizabeth Harrower's *The Watch Tower*, wake no echoes in me.

To raise our family, my husband, Graeme, and I bought a single-storey, double-fronted weatherboard house with a front verandah, a central passage and plenty of sheds. It was as close to an Australian farmhouse as you could get in the inner suburbs, and after we renovated you could see right through from the front door to the back. We still live there, and, as a new grandmother, I imagine our granddaughter exploring the house and garden, making huts, climbing trees, having a little plot to grow radishes and marigolds, poking about in the sheds full of old stuff that might just come in useful one day.

The other gift my grandmother gave me was the past as a lived reality. Because of her, and my grandfather too, I have ended up as a historian, reading old documents, visiting old buildings, looking at photos and paintings of things that once were. There are many reasons for practising history, and some are essentially practical: to study past mistakes and failures so we can try to avoid them, or to uncover the origins of social problems in order to find solutions. Others are more personal: to understand the people who shaped us and what made them, the places they lived in and the textures of their daily lives.

Grandparents are a doorway back into history. Their stories of childhood and school, work and war, and of our own parents' childhood and youth convince us that time is real, and full of consequences. Even if they are not storytellers, their very existence tells us that things were once different and that we too will one day be old like them, if we live that long.

There are, too, the rich pleasures of detailed remembering—Proust's madeleine triggering the recreation of a lost world. Sitting in the archives, reading old letters, I can drift into reverie: the cursive handwriting, the deckle-edged bond paper, the embossed house name in the top right-hand corner evoke the solid confidence of middle-class homeowners and their carless streets. I wonder what the writer's house was like, and what they were wearing when they wrote the letter. Some psychoanalysts talk about reparation fantasies, the need to believe that one can repair a loved one damaged by one's own destructive impulses. I don't think this is what drives my need to remember. It is rather the ravages of time itself that I want to undo as I try to keep the people I love from disappearing.

Both Graeme and I struggle to throw things out. Not for us the joys of decluttering or of the clear desk. Graeme feels he is betraying where he came from if he throws out a broken appliance, so he puts it in the shed to fix later, and occasionally he does. I just feel sad and can only move things out of the house by becoming cross and accusatory: this was always a mistake; I never really liked the person who gave me this; it is tripping me up. Sometimes I do pass things on for their own good: I'm not looking after you, so you should go to someone who will, before neglect renders you useless.

In our house, only the beds, the whitegoods, the computers and the artwork were bought new. The tables, the chairs, the couch, the coffee table, the piano, some of the cupboards, and much of the china, cutlery and glassware all had lives before us: some in my parents' mid-century modern lounge room, the brown furniture in earlier interiors. We have the butter churn from Graeme's family's farm, and a cane washing basket big enough for a sleeping baby, which my grandmother bought at a clearing sale in the 1920s. Then there's the dress archive in the trunk, special dresses of mine and a few of my mother's, like her printed linen 1960s sheath with a keyhole at the neck-line.

The house contains it all, and we are never bored. Graeme always has things to mend, and I can read or sort: my parents' courtship letters, old photos, wooden boxes of costume jewel-lery my sister and I once wore. And if I run out of memory prompts in the house, there is always the garden, where I can weed around my grandmother's violets and white flags, divide the irises from my childhood home, or strike cuttings from my mother-in-law's Jerusalem sage for my daughters to plant in their gardens.

So there will be plenty of paths back to past ways of doing things for little Helena, should she be so inclined. Of course, she may not be; she may want to throw balls, keep guinea pigs and play the ukulele, or do a myriad of other things that don't need my kept objects. But the possibility has given me another reason not to throw things out. Little Helena could play shops with these old pennies, or dress-ups with these old necklaces and stoles, or push the dog around in the 1950s white wicker pram my parents bought when I was born and Graeme restored as a surprise Christmas present after it had spent decades in the old chook shed.

Recently, though, and increasingly, the pleasure of remembering is being overshadowed by my horror at environmental destruction and by my anger that it is continuing almost unabated. My grandparents' farm was on Yorta Yorta land near Kyabram, an Aboriginal word meaning 'thick forest'. Well, there was no thick forest in my childhood, nor native grasses, nor marsupials, just cows, and the occasional native daisy—billy buttons, my father called them. There were birds: carolling magpies, grass parrots, and spoonbills, herons and ibis when the paddocks were being irrigated, the occasional quail, perhaps even a plains wanderer, though I never saw one. But there are a lot fewer birds now. When I drive through Gippsland I mourn the temperate rainforest that once grew there, before the settlers with their fire and axes. And it still goes on: landclearing in Queensland, logging in old-growth forests in Tasmania and Victoria, the draining of wetlands to build coastal housing, the chopping down of eight-hundred-year-old trees sacred to the Djap Warrang people to widen a highway in western Victoria. On and on. On and on. It fills me with despair. What will be left when Helena is my age?

I have never been any good at imagining the future. For a short time in the early 1970s, I had a job in the long-term planning section of Telecom, the statutory organisation that once provided Australia's telecommunications, before it was privatised. I was in a team of social scientists assessing the possible social impacts of advances in telecommunications. It was a job for which I was temperamentally totally unsuited. When the engineers extolled the benefits of 'the wired city', I saw loss: deserted shopping centres, as people shopped online, old ladies forlornly pushing their shopping jeeps, looking for someone to talk to.

In 1975, the planning section, which I had now left, published a report called *Telecom 2000* and I wrote an essay about it for the 1980 *Melbourne Journal of Politics*. I now had a daughter, which gave me another way of imagining the future. She would be twenty-one in the year 2000, I wrote, 'a comforting thought, for it gives a human meaning to the techno-logical future...It reassures that the cyclical time of generations will continue as the linear time of technology speeds on.'

In 'Science as a Vocation', the great German sociolo-gist Max Weber wrote about Leo Tolstoy brooding on the meaning of death in the modern world. According to Weber, Tolstoy concluded that progress had rendered our individual deaths meaningless, that because there is always a further step ahead on the path of progress, the individual life, according to its own meaning, should never end. By contrast, writes Weber, 'Abraham or some peasant of the past died "old and satiated with life because he stood in the organic cycle of life; because his life...had given to him what life had to offer...Civilised man, placed in the midst of continuous enrichment of culture by ideas, knowledge and problems, may be "tired of life" but not "satiated with life".'

I am not as sure as Weber that the organic cycle of life has lost its meaning. Our experience of time moves both in straight lines and in loops and circles; we adapt to external changes and live with chains of consequence, but we also move through the generational positions. Recently my ninety-five-year-old father moved in with us. He sits snoozing and reading in the corner of our lounge, in the chair my mother's mother sat in when she lived in his and my mother's house in my childhood. He still has his mild and gentle manner, but dementia is eroding his agency. I care for him, because he was a good husband and father, but also because he is my grandmother's eldest, much-loved son drifting into a second age of dependency. And when Helena toddles into the lounge, he waves to her, and she waves back.

Nor am I as confident as Weber was about progress and the 'continuous enrichment of ideas'. I fear instead that we are living in an age of decline and endings. There are many strands to this fear: the way the human brain is changing as screens replace books, for instance, and the reappearance of fools and liars with political power, after we thought democracy had saved us from mad kings and queens and their venal courtiers. But my worst fear by far is an existential dread of unstoppable changes to the climate. It haunts everyone I know. It is where the external linear time of nature intersects with the circular time of our generation and those who will follow.

Not everyone feels this fear yet. Most are ignorant of the dangers we face. Some are in denial: all those mad old men who believe in cryogenics and put their brains and bodies into deep freeze, waiting for science to discover how to revive them. And men and women in power, who could lead the world into a carbon-free future, but who are barely able to lift their eyes beyond the next electoral cycle.

So what can a grandmother do?

She can join the climate movement, go to demonstrations, write letters to politicians, sign petitions, donate to environmental organisations. But what can she do for her granddaughter in a world in which she, the grandmother, feels increasingly helpless? She can't protect her from the future. She can't guarantee her the seven decades of post-war peace and prosperity in which she was lucky enough to spend her life. All she can do is give her a house to remember, in which she knows that she was loved.

Jenny Macklin

A Thoroughly Modern Grandmother

On a warm Sunday evening in Melbourne in early 2017, I went about the same routine I'd had for the past twenty-one years. I gathered my papers, packed my clothes and swimmers in my carry-on suitcase (red leopard-print hard case, if you're wondering) and kissed my partner, Ross, goodbye, before heading out the door. It was the start of yet another parliamentary sitting week, so I was off to Canberra to see all my colleagues.

What made this evening so memorable was the wonderful news I had received that day—I was going to be a grandmother. Now, anyone who knows me—heck, anyone who meets me just once will attest to my love of babies. So to hear my son Louis tell me I was going to be a grandmother brought a smile to my face that lasted through all the Question Times that week—no easy feat!

While the news itself didn't surprise me, I was surprised by how deeply thrilled I was about my future grandchild. The happiness in my son's eyes when he shared the news with Ross and me recalled the elation I had felt years before, staring into those same blue eyes when Louis was just a newborn. I knew the exquisite and unique joy that was about to overwhelm him with the birth of his own child, and it made my heart swell.

On that flight to Canberra, I turned the word 'grand-mother' over and over in my mind. What did it mean to be a grandmother? How much would I be involved in the day-to-day life of our grandchildren? What would be too much? Too little? What would be the right balance for me between work and family now that a Macklin grandchild was on its way into the world? I also began to think about all the grandmothers I had met over the years who had profoundly shaped my view of the world. And of course, I thought about my own grandmothers, Grace and Doris.

The lives of my grandmothers were vastly different from mine. Grace and Doris never knew each other, and, unfortunately, I didn't get the chance to know them. They lived far away, and both died before they were seventy. Both were born in Australia at the end of the nineteenth century. Although these years marked the start of significant change for women in Australia and across the world, my grandmothers' own lives were very hard.

My paternal grandmother, Grace, was born in the town

of Clermont, in rural Queensland. Her birth came two years after that of the Australian Labor Party, which took place down the road in Barcaldine at the Tree of Knowledge in 1891. There were no women present at this important gathering. By the time Grace was three, however, South Australia led the world by passing legislation that not only allowed women to vote, but also to stand for parliament. My maternal grandmother, Doris, was born in the similarly tough western suburbs of Melbourne.

The formal educational and employment opportunities available to my grandmothers were scarce. The age of consent in the 1890s was thirteen, and education for girls seldom went beyond the primary years. Work both outside and inside the home was hard and the patriarchal culture was alive and well. Life for most Australian women was exceedingly difficult.

It would have been impossible for them to imagine the life to be led by one of their granddaughters. That this girl—me— would finish school, attend and graduate from university, be elected to the Australian parliament, become deputy leader of the Australian Labor Party, and go on to be the longest-serving woman (so far) in the House of Representatives would have been completely and utterly beyond their comprehension. But it wasn't about their abilities or desires; there was no opportunity for them to choose such a life for themselves.

Am I and the women of my generation, the grandmothers of now, doing enough to ensure the world offers our grandchildren as many opportunities as we experienced?

Grace and Doris did get a chance to do what their own

grandmothers never did: vote in federal and state elections. But their lives remained tough. Paid maternity leave would have been a completely foreign concept to these women, who focused on raising their nine children each and running their households on low incomes with little to no support from outside their families.

But the wheels of change had started to turn and women of all ages and backgrounds worked together to improve other women's future life chances. Most women I know of my generation are acutely aware of the battles fought and won by women before us, and have a great deal of gratitude to our grandmothers' generation.

Coming of age in the 1970s, I was caught up in the wave of women's liberation, which shaped me as a young adult. Many women encouraged and supported me. I believed I could do anything, go to university, study economics, go on to have a long career and have children. I eagerly followed the Whitlam government's progressive agenda: the Equal Pay case, placing the contraceptive pill on the Pharmaceutical Benefits Scheme, paid maternity leave for public servants and, of course, free university education. I got involved in the collective that ran one of the early women's refuges in Canberra.

My friends and I celebrated Whitlam's appointment of a woman, Elizabeth Reid, as a senior adviser on Women and Families. Although this appointment, the first of its kind, was ridiculed in the media—candidates were depicted as swim-wear models—it had a major influence on me and contributed to my decision to head into public policy and politics.

I have run the full gauntlet when it comes to politics. I have won. I have lost. I have had hopes and dreams smashed in an instant and golden opportunities appear out of what felt like nowhere—sometimes all within the same parliamentary sitting week. Through all that, I never lost either my belief in the power of public policy to change lives for the better, or my understanding of how individuals can make a significant difference.

•

My decision to retire from politics in 2019 was nowhere near as tough as I once thought it would be. In truth, it was an easy decision. With two grandchildren now, and perhaps more to come, I could see a new life filled with love, joy and play. Being a grandmother is fun. Of course, I still worry about my kids and my grandkids, but the passing of the baton of responsibility to my son takes the burden off caregiving and opens room for so much joy. And not surprisingly, like many grandmothers, I'm still working outside the home. I know, however, that my experience doesn't necessarily reflect that of many other Australian grandmothers.

Ross did a lot of the day-to-day parenting while I spent much of my children's formative years in parliament, so it is no surprise that he has also taken on a very active role as a grandparent. One of the delights is that we have the time to be with our granddaughter together, to smile at each other as she says something funny or parrots our every word. When our grandson becomes a little less attached to his mother's breast, I trust that he will join us on our trips to see the giraffes and the butterflies at the Melbourne Zoo. We are spreading our wings to include trips to the museum and the local swimming pool, as well as baking banana bread on 'grandparent days'. Already I'm realising that the precious long days before school starts are short-lived and need to be enjoyed as much as possible. As I had limited time with each of my own children during these early years, I'm planning to make the most of them as a grandmother.

My granddaughter is currently in childcare two days a week, while her parents (and grandparents) go to work. I know this isn't an option available to all Australian families. The lack of affordable formal childcare means that many grandparents take on the part-time or full-time care of their grandchildren while the parents go to work. Once the early years are over, this can also mean being available for before-school and after-school care, getting them to after-school activities, and even being on duty over the weekend. This was one of the most highly valued contributions my own parents, John and Vera, made in their nurturing and care of their grandchildren, my children, Josie, Louis and Serge. While I'm sure this is a cherished time for most grandparents, I've also seen close-up the physical, mental and financial burden it can place on many other grandparents.

•

From my own experience of twenty-three years as the member for Jagajaga and a cabinet minister, a number of grandmothers stand out for having given me not only the ideas, but the strength to pursue real and lasting policy changes. They are: Nanna Fejo, Marie Coleman, the survivors of child abuse in institutions, Rhonda Galbally and Rita Beckman.

Nanna Fejo is a Warumungu woman who featured in former prime minister Kevin Rudd's 'National Apology to the Stolen Generations'. Kevin had only been prime minister for two months and was struggling to muster his words and feelings for the Apology. So much rested on it. So many people needed it to reflect their experience, and so many other people needed to understand it. Many people had told him what they wanted to hear, but he also wanted to speak with someone who could describe what happened to children who had been stolen. Just days before the speech was delivered, we contacted Nanna Fejo. Against the odds, she happened to be in Canberra, down from Darwin, visiting her grandchildren. I asked if she would have a cup of tea with the prime minister and me and talk about the Apology. Surrounded by her grandchildren in her daughter's loungeroom, she instinctively knew what the prime minister needed and, through him, what the nation needed.

> *Sometime around 1932 when she was about four, she remembers the coming of the welfare men. Her family had feared that day and had dug holes in the creek bank where the children could run and hide...The kids were found; they ran for their mothers screaming but they could not get away...Tears flowing, her*

mum tried clinging to the sides of the truck as her children were taken away...Nanna Fejo never saw her mother again. Kevin Rudd, 'National Apology to the Stolen Generations', 13 February 2008.

Nanna Fejo and I met up a year later near her birthplace at Tennant Creek, in the Northern Territory. She put a necklace of beads over my head and gave me a note that said thank you. It is impossible to describe what that meant to me.

The second grandmother who influenced me is Marie Coleman, chair of the National Foundation for Australian Women's Social Policy Committee. Government-funded paid maternity leave had been on my agenda for many years, but not so for some of my parliamentary colleagues. Marie's tireless campaigning for paid maternity leave was crucial in influencing my cabinet colleagues in the Labor government to agree to commit to Australia's first paid parental leave scheme in 2009. As the Minister for Families and 'parent' of the scheme, I did not find it an easy conversation at the cabinet table. Finding $731 million over five years in the federal budget following the global financial crisis was a big ask. My 'baby' was born on 1 January 2011, and I'm so proud that the scheme Marie and I dreamed of, and then created, with the help of many others, has since helped 1,065,398 families.

Other grandmothers who significantly influenced my policy-making include those who campaigned for the children who were abused in institutions. Almost 500,000 children were placed in state- or church-run orphanages between the 1920s and 1970s, often because they were living in poverty. The children were the defenceless victims of exploitation, brutality, sexual abuse and neglect. As adults, they rightly demanded a National Apology. This group of grandmothers introduced me to hundreds of those who had been abused. I listened to their stories across the country. I cried a lot while hearing all they had suffered as children and endured over the years into adulthood. I met the families of many more of these Australians who never lived to see the National Apology on 16 November 2009. The toll of the abuse they had experienced in institutional care was too great. There are not enough adjectives to convey the tenacious drive of these grandmothers to bring about significant change, especially given how much pain and suffering they had themselves experienced at the hands of cruel custodians. It was because of them that Julia Gillard, as prime minister, established the Royal Commission into Institutional Responses to Child Sexual Abuse that showed the truth about the abuse meted out to so many Australian children.

Rhonda Galbally never fails to share the latest news about her grandchildren with me. She fits those stories around her powerful advocacy for the rights of people with disability. Her example of combining grandmothering with important political and social-justice work helped guide me as we drove the creation of the National Disability Insurance Scheme. It was Rhonda who led the work that delivered the 'Shut Out' report, outlining how people with disabilities in Australia are 'shut out' from everyday life. It was Rhonda Galbally who knew that, if Australia was to deliver the National Disability Insurance Scheme, differences between carers, people with disability and service providers would have to be put aside and an alliance formed. And that's just what happened. The best grassroots campaign ever created, Every Australian Counts, grew out of this alliance. And now Rhonda is a member of the Royal Commission into Violence, Abuse, Neglect and Exploitation of People with Disability, as well as being a proud grandmother.

Another grandmother who made sure her voice was heard and acted upon is Queenslander Rita Beckman. An important issue I dealt with during my time as a shadow minister was that of grandparents who, mostly due to circumstance rather than choice, are the primary carers of their grandchildren. For those on a pension looking after school-aged grandchildren, the Family Tax Benefit makes a huge difference in their ability to put food on the table and pay any extra school fees and other costs associated with raising children. In 2014, the Labor opposition had to fight a proposal from the then prime minister, Tony Abbott, to remove the Family Tax Benefit (Part B) for families once their children turned six. This would have had a significant impact on more than 4000 grandparent carers of children. Much to Mr Abbott's surprise, a huge number of grandparents across Australia responded by telling very personal stories of their lives as carers. I will always remember the letter Rita Beckman sent me, detailing her shock and rage at the dismissive attitude of the then Minister for Social Services, Christian Porter. She contacted me following Minister Porter's claim in question time that grandparents should effectively see the cut in FTB entitlements as an opportunity to 'go and get a job'. Rita wrote:

> *He [Porter] has assumed that it is easy for grandparents to return to work, even mentioning a number of grandparents who are in the Parliament. I have always worked and paid my way. I am a single aged pensioner and I am the legal guardian for my 10-year-old granddaughter since the sudden death of my daughter. She has been in my care since she was 5 years of age. I am now 75 years old and…I will be 78 when she turns 13 and 81 when she turns 16. I do not wish to seem complaining as I love having this little girl in my life but for goodness sake, how can anyone possibly think an employer would take me on. The arrogance of the Minister for Social Services is breathtaking.*

Rita's voice was supported by a constant stream of grandparents and advocates coming to Canberra and to federal MPs' offices across the country, demanding to know why they were being targeted. What a great demonstration of grassroots political action it was when the government backed down.

I should also acknowledge the tens of thousands of grandparents who spoke to me about the urgent need to increase the age pension rates, when Labor came to power in 2007. More than one grandmother wrote to me about the struggles they faced living as a single pensioner after the death of their husband. It was their stories that influenced me to design the changes to Australia's age pension so that pensioners living alone received the biggest boost to their bank accounts.

●

I hope the legacy of my time in politics has helped to create a better and fairer Australia for my grandchildren to grow up in. We've made many steps in the right direction, but my experience tells me that if we want our grandchildren to survive and thrive in the years to come, we must be vigilant about issues such as these: equality between men and women is not universal; too many Australians live below or just above the poverty line; the First Australians should have a voice protected in the Constitution. And, of course, climate change is a world-changing issue that will have untold impacts on the ways our grandchildren and their children live and work.

Grandmothers have such a vested interest in the future. We can, and should, stay active and engaged in policy debates. Luckily for me, and for this generation of grandmothers, there are many ways to ensure our voices are heard. Contact and lobby your local member of parliament. Lead or support a campaign for a cause you believe is worth fighting for. Use social media to bring about policy change, as well as to share cute photos of the grandkids. We hold this power in the palm of our hands thanks to modern technology.

As a 'thoroughly modern grandmother' whose life was committed to public policy and social change for good, I have a significant amount of both personal and professional skin in the game. Please join me, grandmothers of Australia and beyond, in writing the next chapter.

And to my own grandchildren, may you know only a better future and have even bigger dreams when you look into the eyes of your own grandbabies.

Cresside Collette

Generation

Mila has just celebrated her second birthday. I look at her in wonder: she is her own United Nations, embodying East and West, North and South, almost all the continents.

Her mother is Chilean, from a tiny town situated well down the strip of a country on its way to Patagonia. She is Mapuche, and Spanish. Perhaps there is a hint of German ancestry. My son teases her about the dubious morality of those who fled Europe after the war.

My son is already a wild mixture of races and religions. His father is Polish and Jewish. I was born in Ceylon, now Sri Lanka, of Dutch Burgher parentage. My surname is Flemish and my father's family migrated from the Maastricht district of Holland. My mother's ancestor, Thomas Gratiaen, came from Brussels in the 1700s to work for the Dutch East

India Company. His former profession is listed as 'singer'. His father was a weaver who owned a tapestry manufactory, a detail of which I am extremely proud, as, centuries later, I am a tapestry weaver myself. I had a Scottish great-grandmother, Agnes Keith. And so the melding goes. And we are now Australian.

I look at Mila and hope that, if she is nurtured, she can be a shining light for the human race, an example of all that is good, tolerant and enlightened.

I am very new at the grandmother game. But what I know is that I feel overwhelming love for this small person's spirit, overwhelming wonder at her smallest achievement. And I think with a new intensity about my own grandmother, who, with a fierce dedication to our welfare, played a significant, daily role in our lives across countries and continents. It is hard to imagine that I could be as consequential in Mila's life as my grandmother was in my brother Adrian's and mine.

Political circumstances in Sri Lanka prompted our migration to Australia in 1962. My brave mother, divorced and with no financial support from my father, decided to take the momentous step to leave her comfortable and substantial social life and bring a seven-year-old and an eleven-year-old and her mother, aged seventy, to a new country in order to consolidate our education in the English language. With the election of a nationalist government in our homeland, the ragged remnants of the colonising Dutch had become irrelevant to the progress of the indigenous Sinhalese, and measures were put in place not only to ensure that Sinhala became the main language of the country, but that only two per cent of university places would be given to Dutch Burghers. Our families had lived there for centuries, performing public service and contributing to the country's cultural development, but we were actively discriminated against. And so what is now termed the 'Burgher exodus' began, and we were first in the queue. If being forced from your home means you are a refugee, then we were refugees.

In Australia at that time, the White Australia policy was in full swing: we had to prove our European descent, our 'whiteness', before being allowed to settle here. Once here, 'assimilation' was the catchcry we adhered to. Nineteen-sixties Australia encouraged newcomers to become homogenised, not to reveal their differences. As Ceylon was part of the Commonwealth, a 'pink' country (as my best friend at school put it) on the map of the world, the adjustment was easy. I had played the same games in the schoolyard, recited the same nursery rhymes and read the same books that bound us all to Mother England and created instant common ground.

My mother had worked first as a journalist and then as an advertising copywriter in Ceylon's first advertising agency. After six weeks in our new country, she found a job in a small agency in Melbourne, where she could showcase her immense talent. Bigger offers followed and she never looked back. In those days, it was unusual to have a full-time working mother; our daily nurturing was the province of our grandmother, who provided food, stability, discipline and unqualified love.

I have to talk about her, mainly for Mila, when she is old

enough to read this. I would like to imagine that she would think about me in the same way I think about my beloved grandmother.

Enid Jean Gratiaen (née La Brooy) was born in Victorian times and her morals were honed in that era. From when I was a very small child, I was trained in obedience, consideration, quietness, patience, kindness. The old English proverb 'Children should be seen and not heard' was my grandmother's mantra. I can remember sitting (quietly!) on the dark, polished, red cement verandah of our Colombo house while she entertained her friends to afternoon tea—taken after four-thirty, when the punishing heat of the day had receded—and listening in silent horror to their litany of ailments and operations, which would haunt me at bedtime when my imagination ran riot.

As loving and nurturing as she was, my grandmother was a fierce disciplinarian. When we lived in Ceylon, she kept a small, hidden cane, which she sometimes used across our legs for the unforgiveable crime of 'insolence', or for telling lies. My brother was a much more spirited child than I was and consequently received more canings. Mercifully, the cane did not cross the Indian Ocean with us. The worst punishment she meted out in Australia was to make us sit silently in a corner for an hour, or to give us the 'silent' treatment over a number of days.

'God' and worship at the high altar of Anglicanism was also very present in our lives in Colombo and in Australia. My grandmother would take me and my brother to the three-hour-long 'passion' service on Good Fridays. I was dressed in my uncomfortable best clothes and was expected to 'behave'. In retrospect, I am amazed at her confidence in me to last the distance without complaint, which I did. I was a compliant little girl.

When my parents were still married, my grandparents lived next door and a gate in the high white wall that separated the houses and gardens allowed easy access between our homes. My parents could be described as 'socialites', each with a brilliant career. My father was a celebrated painter and political cartoonist and they knew everybody. Drinks, receptions and embassy parties dominated their evenings. When I was eighteen months old, my father won a State Department scholarship to tour the USA and my parents set off for six months, leaving me and my brother with my grandparents. My grandmother wrote to them every week on blue aerogrammes, lovingly documenting our development. Mila? If you ever read this, listen! It was my grandmother who supervised my play, nurtured my tastes and toilet-trained me. Psychologists would say that this is the time in a child's life when the strongest bonds are formed. I'm certain that it was during these months that my life was irrevocably linked to my grandmother's.

Once back with my busy parents, in their house, I was fed, bathed and readied for bed by my *ayah*, the woman who looked after me. Then Granny would appear through the gate in the fence to read to me, a ritual that bonded me closer to her than to anyone else. Afterwards, she had to slip away while I was distracted or else the evening would end in tears.

In 1956 our lives changed forever. My parents divorced, and, soon after, my grandfather died of a heart attack. So my mother, brother and I moved next door to live with my grandmother. It was also the year that the government brought in the excluding 'Language Act' that eventually decided our migration to Australia.

As far back as I can remember, my grandmother ran the household. In Ceylon she supervised the servants' tasks, wrote the shopping lists, ordered the food and managed the domestic finances. The 'fish man' and the 'egg man' used to deliver to the house and my grandmother would select the best produce from their display. I remember that each egg had to be tested for freshness by being immersed in a basin of water—if it floated, it was rejected. My favourite was the 'haberdashery man', who turned up once a week with shallow wooden boxes piled high on his head and filled with the most colourful sewing cottons, laces, skeins of embroidery, needles, scissors, elastic, hooks and eyes and press studs, from which my grandmother would select what she needed for the task she loved most: making all our clothes, which she created with imagination and flair—and with exquisite embroidery, hemstitching and pintucking.

In some senses, I owe my career and lifelong passion for tapestry-weaving to my early exposure to handcrafts through my grandmother and great-aunts. I spent my childhood at their feet, sorting through the coloured cottons, wools and ribbons, feeling and knowing the difference between a variety of fabrics, and delighting in the treasures of the button boxes, as my grandmother's sewing machine whirred and my aunts' knitting needles and crochet hooks clicked. They were truly the expert practitioners of the gentle arts, and very early in my life I learned to stitch and embroider under their patient tutelage. I can't wait to teach these things to Mila. From the time she was an infant she has sat on my knee at my loom, tap-tapping at the weft with my bobbin, in observant imitation of the technique of weaving.

•

From my perspective, my grandmother's most significant role and responsibility in life commenced with our emigration. In her seventies, she had to adapt to a purely Anglo-Saxon society and cook for her family every day. In Colombo, she had consulted the *Ceylon Daily News Cookery Book* and served delicious Dutch cakes, treats and sweetmeats by ordering our cook and another servant to weigh, sift, knead and mix ingredients on the marble-topped table on the back verandah. But, as she freely admitted, she didn't know how to boil a potato when she came to Australia. It was our great good fortune that she turned out to be an interested and gifted cook in her own right.

As we grew up in our new country, our grandmother was the constant, stable presence at home, while my mother worked and enjoyed the social life she deserved at her young age. Of course, at the time, we did not even remotely think about how important it was to have someone who loved us so completely, and who could be relied upon so completely to be there at all times, even though, as teenagers, we disagreed with her somewhat narrow opinions and Victorian morals. In the wider world, her grandchildren could do no wrong in her eyes, and she expressed her pride in us in a way my mother never could. For Adrian and me, it was our grandmother who inspired our confidence to be who we aspired to be.

So what do I take of this experience into my own role as a grandmother? Part of me wants to say *everything*. But this can't be true, can it? The two words that spring to mind are patience and presence. And an eye for detail. I believe that it is the appreciation of the details in all we do and experience in life that leads to ultimate satisfaction. Sitting at the feet of my grandmother and great-aunts all those years ago, sorting through all the bits and pieces that were adding up to something else, something more than just the item of clothing being created—that's what taught me how to see.

As the mother of two sons, my heart was captured by the anticipation of a female grandchild. After her mother went back to work part-time, I was privileged to be able to look after Mila one day a week from the age of four months to eighteen months old. When she was tiny, the days were filled with comforting her, providing bottles and cuddles to lull her to sleep. I was in constant wonder at the tiny expressive hands, the exquisite little mouth, the long, dark eyelashes that finally fluttered in submission to resisted rest. Holding her close and observing her every feature gave me the most overwhelming feeling of comfort and purpose—that this was where I was meant to be; that I had arrived at the right destination in my life. Those accumulating wrinkles on my neck were there precisely for her small, searching hands to stroke as she drifted off contentedly in my arms.

As she grows, there is the fun of games. Her interaction and engagement with the world around her is total. She loves the physicality of life. Quick to laugh, she reacts to songs and music with delight and holds a tune convincingly. I want to teach her the songs that I love. She runs rather than walks, unafraid of tumbles. We create our special world, whether we're at her house or mine.

In my sitting room is a low Korean chest that belonged to my mother, in polished wood with brass fittings and three drawers filled with small delights—carved and painted ducks, a menagerie of wooden animals, sea shells, intricate silver boxes, old coins and silk tassels. Mila unloads these trinkets over and over, examining and reconfiguring them, secure in the knowledge that they will be waiting for her every time she visits.

I can recall as a child the delight I felt at being allowed to look at and sometimes touch collections of tiny objects stored by my great-aunts in glass-fronted cabinets. Tiny Delft tea sets and figurines, Dutchmen and women dressed in felted outfits, small plates adorned with windmills. They provided endless child-sized fascination as they imprinted a visual heritage far from our tropical existence. My collection, though different in content, will foster in Mila the ability to respond to the tactility of small objects of wonder that fit into her hand, and an ability to observe them closely.

She loves the repetition of certain activities, and I participate in these with no sense of boredom. I do the simple things with her that her parents are too preoccupied to do. Slow turns around the garden on sunny days, examining every flower, commenting on their colour and variety and picking some for a vase. Blowing the dandelion puffs. Playing with pebbles, dropping them through the holes in the garden furniture on the patio. Sitting still, watching the birds flit through the trees and dance on the roof. Running the hose and filling a watering can to sprinkle the plants. Splashing her hands and placing flowers and concrete birds in the birdbath. Throwing a tennis ball high into the sky and following its wayward trajectory. Jumping in piles of dry leaves to hear them crunch. Together, we appreciate and rejoice in the simplest of things. I learn again what it is to look at life through a child's innocent eyes.

And now her words are tumbling out, mostly English, some Spanish. Both languages have resounded in her psyche from the time she was born. How fortunate she will be bilingual, able to take both languages for granted. Her parents reinforce her awareness of manners and she finds it natural to say please and thank you in her sweet voice.

There are the things I look forward to doing with her in the future. Already she greets me with special joy every time I see her. I hope to build her awareness of the visual world through making paintings and objects, visiting galleries and stimulating her creative imagination. When she is able to concentrate for longer periods, I will read to her from my much-loved library of children's books, which were part of my childhood and which, in turn, I read to my sons. And I will teach her to cook, to savour the tastes that are part of her heritage, and which are so much a part of my own enjoyment of life.

Mila now attends childcare, so I have lost that one precious day a week when I could look after her for an extended time. There is no doubt that she enjoys the interaction with other children and the stimulation of an environment in which she is learning new skills. But I miss not having her possession of me for those hours when we were together, just the two of us, spontaneous in our activities, with little regard for passing time.

I rejoice in the fact that she lives in a country where diversity is recognised and valued, and I trust that the word *assimilation* will continue to disappear from our collective vocabulary. My hopes for her in an uncertain world are coloured by the yearning I have to be present for her at all times, as my grandmother was for me, offering security and protection. As she steps out, sure-footed and completely confident, to make her individual mark upon this world, I will be right behind her.

Célestine Hitiura Vaite

Mo'otua–Grandchild

'Ia ora na i te mahana 'āpī. Hello in the new day.

Every day is a new day.

Allow me to share with you, in English, a Tahitian proverb.

> *The shell of Woman is Woman. It is from Woman,*
> *Woman is born.*
> *The shell of Man is Woman. It is from Woman, Man*
> *arrives in the world.*

I am fifty-three and I have three sons, Genji, Heimanu and Toriki, and a daughter, Turia.

My belly was their shell.

In May 2011, Genji married Angela. Both wanted children, but not straightaway.

My daughter, Turia, was in the prime of her life. She and Michael felt ready for a baby and hoped for a boy. We were having the conversation in the car, on our way to Turia's graduation, three hours' drive to Sydney from the South Coast. She and Michael said they liked the name Billy.

'*Billy?*' The tone in my voice from the back seat said it all. How could my *mo'otua* be named *Billy?*

'Our child, Mum,' said Turia. 'You gave Genji a Japanese name.'

'What about the middle name?' I asked. It was a hypothetical conversation—about Billy Moana Hoskin.

Four days after her graduation in September 2011, Turia was caught in a bushfire during a hundred-kilometre marathon for which she had trained hard. She was in Intensive Care at Concord Hospital, Sydney, not expected to survive. I prayed. I prayed to God. I prayed to the Ancestors.

I even prayed to Billy Moana Hoskin. 'Billy Moana Hoskin, you must be born…One day. Your mother must live.'

In North Sydney, weeks before, Genji and Angela had moved into their two-bedroom apartment. Michael and Genji went out to buy a bed for the spare bedroom. We were all thrown into the chaos. On the balcony, I'd be bawling my eyes out. How could you do this, God? My daughter is a good person. Genji said he didn't believe in God. Could I please stop talking about God?

All that happened over the next six months while Turia

stayed in Concord has already been well documented. Turia's survival was a miracle. We all love miracles. Miracles make good stories.

'Mum. We're all going to the pub,' Genji said.

'*The pub?*' Was my son serious? Did we have something to celebrate? 'I'm not going to the pub.'

'Mum. We're all going to the pub. Turia is going to survive.'

I should have been rejoicing, but I was still too upset about Turia's last operation.

At the pub, Genji played the comedian. He told a story about Billy and Tamatoa, cousins who, one day, would grow up together on the South Coast. Billy would have blond hair flowing in the wind, and would ride his bike with a cockatoo on his shoulder. Billy would come around to see if cousin Tamatoa was keen to surf. Billy would also have his surfboard on his bike. But Tamatoa, with a short military hairstyle like his father, would have to make his bed first, as if he was in the army. We all laughed at Genji's vision of my imaginary future grandchildren.

•

Three years later, Genji called from North Sydney.

'Hey, Mum, how do you say *boy* in Tahitian? And how do you say *girl?*'

'What?' Why? Was there something I should know?

'Can you just tell me,' said Genji, urgently. 'We're at the vet. Ange and I bought two puppies.'

'*Tane*, boy. *Vahine*, girl.' Genji must have forgotten his language once I stopped talking to him in Tahitian, when I was trying to teach myself English.

'How do you spell them?'

'*T-a-n-e*. In Tahitian, the *e* is pronounced é as in café. *V-a-h-i-n-e*.'

'Thanks, Mum!' *Click*. He'd explain later.

The dogs were for Angela, to keep her company. Genji was often away with his job as a clearance diver for the Australian Navy, leaving for classified missions, even overseas.

Tane and Vahine, brother and sister from the same litter, a cross between pug and cavalier. They became the grand-dogs of Ma'u and Pa'u.

I'm Ma'u. Grandma in Tahitian, pronounced *Ma-ou*. My husband John is Pa'u, pronounced *Pa-ou*.

Genji and Angela went to England for Christmas, to see Angela's family, so the grand-dogs stayed on the South Coast and had a ball at the dog-friendly beach.

When was Genji moving to England, asked Angela's mother, Anne, in 2017. She missed her daughter. Genji and Angela said they would try for a baby, then move to England with Tane and Vahine, Angela's babies. Angela wasn't leaving her babies behind. In five years, they'd all come back. In the meantime, they bought an investment property in Mollymook, in Tallwood, around the corner from Michael and Turia in Donlan, which is around the corner from John and me.

But that same year, Genji and Angela broke up. The day I learned of the separation in a phone call from Genji, I remembered Angela had written possible names for children in a love heart on a page in one of my notebooks. I found the notebook straightaway. I couldn't believe it. There they were: 'Tamatoa Christopher Pitt and Leilani Georgia Pitt.' If that had been a sign, it was no longer true…Genji and Angela moved out of their apartment and went their separate ways. Angela took her babies. They remained friends.

●

In 2018, I was at Donlan to say *ia orana*, hello, and have a cup of tea with Turia. Over tea or a meal, we'd talk about many things, have a few laughs. She'd say I was funny. She was too. We'd tell each other we should have our own comedy show.

'Hey, Mum,' said Turia that day in the kitchen. 'Could you get me the yellow scrunchie from my bedside table.'

'Sure.' Too easy.

I looked for the scrunchie. Nowhere to be seen. 'Turia! I don't see a yellow scrunchie!' Did it have to be yellow? Surely not.

She marched to the room, retrieved something from the bedside drawer and showed it to me.

'What's this?' Is this what I think it is? Two lines on a pregnancy test. 'Are you pregnant?'

'Yes.'

'*AH!!!!!!*' I screamed the roof down. 'You could have asked me to sit down!'

'I can't believe you didn't see it, Mum.'

'I wasn't looking for a pregnancy test,' I said. 'So I didn't see it. Have you seen a doctor, darling?'

'I did four pregnancy tests.'

'*Four?*' One would have sufficed, maybe two.

'I wanted to be sure.'

I hugged my daughter tight. 'I'm so happy for you, darling, so happy.'

Michael came into the bedroom. He had gone along with Turia's scheme for me to find out, but it hadn't worked. No drama, he was still smiling.

'Group hug!' said Turia.

•

The name Hakavai means Dance of the Water. He arrived in the world in the season of the gardenias, after the summer rain. I met him twenty minutes after his arrival at Wollongong Hospital. He looked a bit freaked out:

Where am I?

You are in the world. Who are you?

Feeling the love.

'*Ma'ou.*'

My son Toriki, the youngest in the family at twenty, but the tallest, lived in Wollongong, where he was studying electrical engineering. We all gathered at his share house. Genji and Angela had driven to Wollongong, bringing their DJ brother Heimanu.

'Hey, Mum,' said Heimanu. 'How does it feel to be a grandma?' Big hug.

'How does it feel to be an uncle?'

I then hugged my daughter-in-law. 'Hello, Madame Pitt.'

'Hi, Mummastine. It's good to see you.'

'Hey, Mum.' Big hug from Genji. No one really knew if he and Angela were back together, but she was here, and that said a lot to me.

At the hospital Genji and Angela had hogged the baby.

•

In Mollymook, the season of the gardenias returned after the 2019 summer rain. Genji called. They were now back living together in the eastern suburbs of Sydney.

'Hey, Mum, what are you doing for your birthday?'

'My birthday is eight months away.'

'Do you have any plans for your birthday?'

'Why are you talking to me in riddles?'

'I'm talking in riddles, am I?'

'Yes, you are, darling.'

'It's just that…around your birthday…you're going to be a grandma again.'

'Oh my God! Is it true?' I heard Angela chuckle. I was on speaker.

'Hello, Madame Pitt!'

'Hi, Mummastine!'

'I'm so happy for you both! I'm crying.'

'Ange got pregnant straightaway.' Once they had decided on a baby.

'That baby has been waiting years to be conceived!' I was yelling with unrestrained joy. But the move to England was now real. They were leaving in six months. Angela would give birth in the English summer.

Genji asked if they could store some stuff in my garage. He was thinking ahead.

'Of course, darling,' I said. 'From here it'll be easy to transfer your stuff to Tallwood in five years.'

Genji chuckled. I don't miss a beat.

The garage was already chockablock with my stuff, stuff from my three sons, John's sporty memorabilia, Genji's military uniforms, which I couldn't take to Vinnies because it's a crime to impersonate a soldier. And that silly treadmill that Toriki had promised to 'grab next time'.

Months passed, Hakavai was not only walking, but running, a bundle of happy energy. At fifteen months, he had strong legs from all the training at Mollymook Beach. I used to take the mini footy along, a birthday gift from Ma'u and Opa, on Hakavai's first birthday, along with his blue flute and Rubik's Cube. It'll take Hakavai years to work out the Rubik's Cube, but he'll get there.

For years, John was Pa'u with the puppies, when he'd bring treats home in the grocery bag for Tane and Vahine. Guess what Pa'u got you? For three months, John was Pa'u with Hakavai, then Pa'u John had a rethink. 'I'm half-Dutch,' he said. 'I should really be Opa.'

•

Hakavai liked to breathe in and out fast into the 'upa'upa vaha, music music mouth, the mouth harmonica. And he sure loved to dance to the harmonica blues. He was a natural. Check the hips! Then it'd be book time on the couch with Ma'u, reading books that Hakavai had chosen himself at Ulladulla Library, with his own library card.

In England, Grandma Anne had installed the air-con in Genji and Angela's bungalow, in expectation of their arrival.

Genji and Angela had found out that they were going to have a boy. Teiva would be his name. Prince of the Islands.

We come from many islands. The ocean, the world's greatest temple, connecting us.

I'd think of Teiva being born, and feel sad. How could his ma'u, me, teach him Tahitian if he lived in England?

Hakavai already knew a few words. '*Inu.*' Drink. He'd take a few sips of water from his sippy cup. '*Amu.*' Eat. Omelette made with free-range eggs, fresh herbs from the garden, grated parmesan. '*E haere tatou.*' Let's go. Let's go for an adventure on Mollymook Beach. See if we can find bird feathers on the beach. I had already woven pandanus leaves in the shape of a whale that now hung on the wall at home. Bird feathers also make excellent bookmarks and pens to draw with on the canvas of the sand. Now I took Hakavai's beloved soccer ball along. Sorry, Opa Johnny Maguire, former rugby league great. Hakavai prefers soccer.

A surprise call from Genji: 'Hey, Mum, we're not going to England anymore.'

'What happened?'

'The airline rang. Tane and Vahine won't survive the

flight. They'll die.'

So the family was moving to Tallwood.

Angela could continue her brilliant career as a financial adviser. Genji would take leave for a year and be a stay-at-home papa with Teiva. I told my son he had served his country well, both in the army and as a clearance diver.

Genji intended to put native trees in the garden at Tallwood. I immediately suggested lilly pilly trees. 'I'll make lilly-pilly jam.' It was Hakavai's favourite. He helped me pick the berries.

'Yeah, I heard about your lilly-pilly jam! That's good, Mum.'

'Put in some bush tomato plants too, and some lemon myrtle trees.' Hakavai loved the scent of lemon myrtle leaves. And sea rocket, and saltbush, and karkalla.

'Ange would like a few apple trees,' said Genji. 'But what about the birds?'

'*What about the birds?*' I said. Rainbow lorikeets, cockatoos...

'Won't they eat the apples?'

'The birds won't eat all the apples! You want birds in your garden,' I said enthusiastically.

Genji was also visualising a massive veggie garden, pumpkins galore.

Turia was so happy about her brother moving back to the South Coast. They could surf together like they used to as children. Hakavai and Teiva would hang out. Michael and Genji, mates since Ulladulla High School, would go diving for abalone and fish, and surf in the clear South Coast waters.

There is another *mo'otua* on the way.

It was Hakavai who passed the positive pregnancy test to me. *'Ma'ou,'* he said to me, as he hung in his mum's arms.

Turia and Michael were smiling.

I thought it was a thermometer. 'What is he doing with a thermometer?' I snatched it from him.

Surprise!

I hope she will be a girl, Clarity of the Moon.

Anastasia Gonis

Life in the White House

It was summer when we arrived at the white house, half a kilometre from the village and surrounded by olive groves. It stood solid and alone. The branches on the plane trees moved to their own music and the sound of their leaves was carried on the wind as we entered the gate. A cast of eagle hawks circled high above. The fruit trees in the garden were bent with produce. Soon there would be chairs and tables along the marble verandahs.

This was my utopia, the village in the south of Greece from where my husband had migrated sixty years before. We had lived there, in the dream house we had built, for nine years in the eighties, when I had raised my children to adulthood. It was where I felt at home. The warm weather would be therapeutic: my chronic back pain had wearied me and stolen my spark. I was going to finish writing the two books I had begun. I also had plans to create a writers' retreat. For me, at fifty, it would be a time to flourish, to do something that I felt would enhance me. Our three children had built lives of their own and I felt comfortable that we would see each other often—we were, and still are, a family of travellers.

As a child born in Cyprus into a Greek-Cypriot family, regardless of being raised in Australia, I had been taught the fundamentals of what is expected of a woman: family first, no negotiation on that. Then respect and obedience, no negotiation there either. My husband, who had migrated from Greece to Australia when he was twenty years old, longed for his homeland. His homesickness was like a seeping wound. As the core of our family unit, he was my first priority. My primary duty was to him, ahead of our three children. I had travelled between Melbourne and the white house many times in order for him to heal.

When I was forty, and back in Australia after those nine years in Greece, I had enrolled to get my school leaving certificate, determined to fulfil my longing for an education. Five years of a part-time writing course followed. Soon I was publishing articles, stories, poetry, and book and film reviews. I secured a job in a bookshop. Could life have been more perfect? I was a writer. People paid me for my words. Writing, writers and books filled my life. My dreams had come true. I loved the person I had become. I enjoyed attending writing events, and literary festivals. I realised that writers were people like me, who had built their life on words. I never wanted anything to change in the space I had carved for myself.

•

Thirteen months after our arrival at the white house, the call came from our eldest son in Australia. Our first grandchild was on the way. I had never given a thought to being a grandmother. It seemed another stage in life, for later, an end-of-life thing. I was wrapped up in the excitement and challenge of the present, of my writing projects.

My husband and I realised we couldn't stay away. Our children and grandchildren would need us. And we wanted to be there. I left my projects and dreams locked in that white house and travelled back in time; I pretended that I hadn't left Australia at all, that living again in Greece had been an illusion. I made the decision based on what I had been taught: that a mother always makes sacrifices for her family.

•

Arriving back in Australia, I remembered other key moments in my life. I saw myself at fourteen beneath the flowering plum tree in the backyard of our house in Melbourne—with my exercise book, a pencil and a dreamy feeling. There I was, thinking about red lipstick and velvet skirts, embroidered vests, coloured scarves and lace-up boots, the clothes I would wear one day, as a writer. I used to imagine myself sitting at a desk, papers lifted by the breeze coming through a window that filled my study with light. My writing place would have solitude and nature, the sound of the wind in the trees. That is where I would write my stories.

When I was a teenager, the young Anglo girls in my neighbourhood had boyfriends; some had babies very young, which their mothers looked after while they continued on with their lives. Those girls had laughed at the Greek-Cypriot traditions and customs by which I had been raised—they found them strange and inhibiting. I was torn. I, too, found many of our traditions restrictive, and resented the obedience expected of me, but I adhered to that principle instilled in me by my mother: family first.

My head was always buried in a book. I dreamed of going to Mac.Robertson Girls' High School, the government-funded, academically selective secondary school in Melbourne, because that was the school for clever girls. I was filled with joy and hope by my father's encouragement: I was 'his only child who loved learning'. My mother had other ideas. We were four girls in the family. That meant trouble. Mum's best friend was our local priest's mother. Marry them off early was her sour advice, which my mother took as gospel. Her religious beliefs dictated her actions. Marriage would protect us from the world outside the family circle.

Not long after my thirteenth birthday, my father told me that, for financial reasons, he needed me to leave school and go to work. It was the last thing I wanted, but I obeyed without question. Family first...Three years later I was married.

Another key moment that came back to me was when my younger sister returned to Cyprus with my parents. At seventeen she married a Cypriot man and stayed there. Carer for my blind mother until both our parents passed away, she had also shifted smoothly into the role of carer for her own children's children, raising them as her own. She was always available to them, day and night. Any dreams she may have had for herself dissolved. Was I destined to follow her example?

I made the decision to come home as an onlooker only in my children's new lives as parents. I fully intended to continue with my ambitions as a writer.

•

And I did not object in the slightest to being included in everything: the exercise classes, shopping for the baby, doctor's visits, the whole package that came with the pregnancy. I was excited about the arrival of this new family member. I loved him/her already.

When the pains started early that Greek Easter morning, we spent the entire day in the birthing room—and all our lives changed.

When I held my grandson, a transformation occurred. A fierce love swept through me, an awakening quite unlike the one I experienced at the birth of my own children. I recalled the Greek adage: *The child of my child is twice my child*. I felt that, with this new baby, I could begin to make amends for the ignorance of my youth. I had always thought I had failed my children because I hadn't known enough at the time. I had been a child myself, selfish and unpredictable, trying to raise children. I remembered myself as a young girl giving birth in a hospital, all alone. How did I survive that? Why did it happen that way? And who was I all those years ago? Had my experiences in any way prepared me for the role that I had now chosen? I couldn't yet tell.

The shift in my life came so quickly: I stepped into the role of grandmother as if into a new dress. It seemed the most beautiful dress I had ever owned. I seemed to glow within the light created by this child. The days were filled with activity and I tapped resources within me to do whatever was needed. I cared for and loved this new life. I grew into someone else as he grew and changed under my care.

J was one of those babies who never slept during the day except in the moving pram and for very short periods of time. I would walk him around the streets of my suburb for hours. I took him everywhere with me. His company filled the space my writing had once occupied. He was a quiet and intelligent child who grasped language and concepts quickly. He became my fourth child. How had I ever imagined being an onlooker?

Then my second grandchild, M, was born. My daughter spent the first year at home minding him. By this time J was ready for school. I willingly chose to shift from carer of one child to carer of another. Family first. My lineage was secured. What I had done for the first I had to offer to the next. My intention was to maintain harmony in the family, especially between my children. I had seen too many families fall out over grandparents not sharing their childminding time equally between their children. My own family had been far from a showcase in this area.

My daughter was Wonder Woman, capable and independent. In my opinion, however, it was to her detriment that she avoided extending the hours I had M. She was always on time and pedantic about not asking for extra help from me, no matter how stretched she was. I realise now how thoughtful she was, viewing the situation through the eyes of both a mother and a daughter. Her father called her a feminist. He'd always disapproved of empowered women. But there was a twinkle in his eye when he said it, for he secretly admired her grit. I called her headstrong, a tenacious perfectionist who was also very much like me.

M was a captivating child, full of curiosity, energy and imagination. He'd move from one project to another, trying to fit a week's play into a day. His thirst for learning was insatiable. We moved incessantly from dress-ups to playing shop, from building with icy-pole sticks to drawing, from books to puzzles.

Although my days were monotonous and without any intellectual stimulation, I delighted in the fact that I was an influential instrument in these new lives, that I was creating memories for them to take into the future. I felt central. I felt useful. And this gave me a new identity. I measured my learning against my teaching and found it hard to ascertain who benefited more.

The third grandchild—my daughter's second child was born and my performance continued. D was a quiet, undemanding child. His concentrated and uninterrupted play made him at times seem invisible. He especially loved it when we did baking together. I taught him how to roll out the perfect biscuit, by straightening his fingers and rolling the dough using his palms until it was the desired thickness. Then he would form a figure eight and set it on the tray with the correct space between each one. This was and still is his preferred activity.

I loved my grandchildren so much, but I was starting to have serious health issues again with my back and could not always be available. I was literally 'wearing out'. Childcare facilities were hard to get into, although it wasn't through lack of trying. I was so desperate that I went to the childcare centre and broke down: I begged we be given priority at the first available opening. Two weeks later, we heard back from them and, just like that, my carer's hours were halved. My house was still where children were dropped off and picked up regularly, but childminding was no longer what consumed my life.

Many times through those years of caring for my grandchildren, I longed for my old life, when I could sit and read, write and dream. When I felt overwhelmed by the small children, I dreamed of running away. I wouldn't tell anyone; I'd just go to a secret place I'd chosen. I even researched country towns in Victoria. I looked up train timetables. These escape plans were mad, but they gave me an outlet when the pressures of responsibility made me afraid of what would happen if I somehow failed to look after these children properly. In the meantime, I continued to oil the wheels of my children's daily existence.

Finally, all the boys were at school. There were only the school drop-offs and pick-ups. My writing had, by now, all but stopped. The few reviews, articles or interviews I did were without pay, but I was determined not to disappear into the ether, although I thought many times about giving up writing altogether. I re-entered the race, a straggler, at the end of the line, attempting to pick up pace and move towards the destiny I had once chosen for myself.

I began to attend literary events again. I tried to return to the books I had started writing so long ago, but just couldn't reignite the spark. Writing needs emotional energy. Mine was extinguished. I no longer had the passion or persistence to regain a foothold in the small writing community I had once been part of.

Being a grandmother had consumed me. Although I had more time now, and seemed to spend a lot of it with books, the life I had imagined for myself in my late forties and early fifties was no longer attainable. The race was not yet over, but the stakes had changed. To be happy or at least content again, I had to reconcile who I was then with the person I had become.

•

In Greece once again, some months after my sixty-fifth birthday, while sitting on the verandah beneath the glow of stars, the sound of cicadas flooding the air, trying to identify the direction of the jackals' howls coming from the bushes and gullies, I took a call from our youngest son in Australia.

Another grandchild on the way. This was wonderful news for all of us because he and his wife had been married for ten years and they were not sure pregnancy would happen for them. Along with the joy, I couldn't help but reflect on the drastic change that awaited them; I wondered how they would manage after a life of travel and ease.

It had been nine years since I had cared for a newborn. I had changed, as had my energy levels, physical endurance and headspace. The continuous therapies for my chronic pain had played havoc with my mind; there were empty spaces where knowledge and experience should have been. Regardless, on our return to Australia from our holiday in Greece, I was prepared to help with this child as well.

Another boy! For six weeks, I spent twelve hours each day, except weekends, at my son's place. Once at home, I would go straight to bed and start again the next day. There was no time for thought, let alone analysis of my life. After the initial difficulties of forming a routine of feeding and sleeping for the baby, life smoothed out for us all. When my daughter-in-law returned to part-time work, I again reverted to the role of carer, mostly at my son's place. I shifted rather tentatively into the role I had felt in the past I was good at. It wasn't an easy transition. I felt anxious and fearful at times because I had lost confidence in my ability to be what my children expected of me. As time passed and this grandchild grew into a walking and talking toddler full of curiosity and animation, I drew on that incredible surge of love that was mine the day I held my first grandchild.

Any plans to return to Greece for a lengthy stay became unattainable, for our lives became dependent on our children's and grandchildren's needs. Short stays for rejuvenation became our yearly pilgrimages.

Now that I have time to consider my contribution as a grandmother, I have decided that it was indeed necessary and valuable. Because of my passionate belief that family came first, I saw myself as the solution to any struggles my children experienced as parents. I watched my sons wrestle with work commitments while sharing the parenting role and the accompanying sleep deprivation. I knew my daughter was always stretched to the limit, but there was only so much I could offer. I continued to feel guilty and believed that perhaps I should or could have done more for them all.

Instead of accepting the enrichment that being a grandmother offered, however, I had often felt cheated. I wouldn't let go of the grievance I felt for what had happened to that dreamy young girl full of promise, reading a book beneath a plum tree all those years ago. She saw herself as a writer, but couldn't see all the other things that would make up the rich texture of her life, the reality of family. Just as, later, I couldn't envisage what the role of a grandmother entailed, and so cheated myself of the wonder that came with being one.

But I made those choices, and now I can look back and examine the different identities and roles I took on, especially now that I have retrieved a portion of my writing life, which I protect with reinforced armour. The race continues. A grandmother is me at my most authentic now.

The white house is now painted different colours. It reflects the changes we have undergone over the last sixteen years. The exterior is a light grey with dark grey trim. The inside walls of the living area are painted a rich Indian red; the bedrooms are blue and cream. The verandahs remain open to the elements.

The eagle hawks—*koufo gerakines* in Greek—still circle the house and now make their nests in the giant oak tree in the yard. The fruit trees grow taller and stronger with time. It is still our utopia, awaiting our return.

Katherine Hattam

Grandmothering and Art

The plan is to wake up early and finish writing about the unexpected pleasures of grandmothering delightful Penelope. Penelope is almost a year old. I set the alarm for six a.m, but my phone pings at five with a wonderful photograph of Lucky. Lucky is just hours old. There is also a photo of his beautiful, exhausted mother. I am now a grandmother of two.

I am new to this. Having a gynaecologist and obstetrician father who often warned against being 'an elderly prima-gravida' meant I wasn't one. I had two sons, Charlie and Will, in my twenties and a daughter, Harriet, at thirty-four. But, unlike me, my sons have waited until their forties to repro-duce, and Harriet is currently an observant and doting aunt.

But there's the geographical interference. Penelope in Geelong, Lucky in Ibiza, Spain, me in Thornbury, Melbourne.

My grandchildren are semi-virtual. But the themness of these two overrides that. And the iPhone has new significance. All our lives have been changed forever by the new technology, but never in my imaginings and planning for becoming a grandmother did I predict the importance of my phone. I am able to see and hear them in a daily way that would once only have been possible had we all lived in a country town or local suburb, across the road rather than across the world. Where would I be without these photographs, videos and FaceTimes? They deal with the geography and I watch and re-watch the videos.

Yes, my eye is my first sensor, but then there are those sounds. Lucky coos, struggling intensely to mimic his parents, and now, at three months, with enormous cheeks and sparkling eyes, he almost talks. This is what the short, intimate videos from the other side of the world tell me. And I can hear Penelope discussing with herself where to drag the adult-sized watering can as, with determination, she follows her father about his Sunday gardening in the sun. But the phone does not give me touch—the softness of her skin is not translated through to my fingers or lips. And when they look at the phone, they do not see me. The all-important eye contact is absent. I am the watcher. The grandmother watching them change.

Occasionally I have, misguidedly, thrust my phone at someone who turns out to be oblivious to the pleasure and importance of that smile or those first steps, and I am embarrassed to admit I'm known to have forwarded photographs of my grandchildren as if they were 'Madonna and Child' paintings by Raphael. Of my siblings, I'm the first to have grandchildren and they appreciate and are indulgent with my infatuation. I was slightly taken aback, though, when I remarked to one of my sisters how beautiful a newborn grandchild was and she replied, matter-of-factly: 'All babies are.' I suppose they are. I look at all babies differently now.

In contrast, the other grandmother, mother of the beautiful, exhausted mother, understands my adoration exactly. She was there in Ibiza when Lucky was born and could fill in details of the birth and agree with me about this boy's extraordinary beauty.

Being a grandmother is a new stage of life for me. I see it is a version of being a parent—an upgraded version, perhaps? I know things now I didn't know, could not have known at twenty-four, when my first son was born.

Instantaneous birth photographs that ping on my phone in the dawn—what a contrast to the way I did it. A hospital photographer brought me a sheet of images of my baby, who was in an institutional cot in the nursery down the corridor. I chose which photographs to buy, and how many of each. Once home from hospital, I mailed the prints to family and friends. It was a slow process, but it did have the advantage of enabling privacy for the new family.

I have always had a strong sense of responsibility and have always fitted my work as an artist around my children. I was a teacher, I cared for my parents, and recently I cared for my husband Jim, who died three weeks before Penelope was born.

(Death and birth often happen coincidently like that.) And so, muddled in with the grief, after a happy forty-year marriage, was the inkling that I could now put my work first. Did I feel guilty, thinking like this? Strangely, realistically, I didn't. Freud said you need two things to make happiness happen: work and love. Work was an important shared part of our life together and it was what remained.

So, when anticipating Penelope's birth, I found myself worrying that I would have to be involved, that the new parents would need my help. I didn't quite want to examine how helping them would fit in with my work. Then I saw Penelope, and held her, and my anxiety evaporated in an instant.

Penelope's father, Charlie, suggested I might come and stay one night a week. What a change that was from when, some years before her birth, I had said to him, 'I'd like to speak to you once a week,' and he had replied, shocked, 'Oh no, that's way too often.'

I was better prepared with the as yet un-held Lucky. By then I had over a year of practice at being a grandmother. And I knew that a new young person in the family would change everything for the better. As Charlie said: 'It's a shared positive.'

Since becoming a grandmother, I have looked back at myself, not just as a mother but as a child. It is a pathway to the past that is mainly visual, because, like most families, we have photographs. There we are on tricycles, in the paddling pool, at the beach. I am the oldest of four, three girls each fifteen months apart, a seven-year gap and then a boy.

When brother John, the baby, arrived, my father bought a movie camera, but I can only recall one film. It was of baby John waking up. Because the print of the film has been lost, it is only running in my memory, unlike the paintings of us by my father, and the photographs of the three girls by fashion photographer Helmut Newton. My mother, unusually for those days, worked full-time, as the advertising manager at the high-end, fashionable Melbourne department store, Georges. She worked with Newton, so he photographed us, naked in the garden amid daisies (that photographer with the three little girls might be seen differently now). When the middle sister asked our mother where we were living when the next sister was born, our mother replied, 'I have no idea.' It says a lot about her state of mind and her life at the time with a full-time job and three children under four.

Significant as the photographs are, my sister's primary-school diary is a key piece of non-visual evidence about my unusual and early duties of care. One entry explains something to me. When our mother asks my sister to give John a bottle, she replies: 'Can't Katherine do it?' 'No,' says Mum, 'Katherine has already given us tea and toast in bed.' The oldest child is marked in a different way from the others. I was nine and already taking on responsibilities.

Work, love and responsibility have jostled for my time since I was very young, and the urgency of my work, something I always felt, has persisted into grandmotherhood. Art, creative work, is reparative, but it demands selfish time, and getting time for myself, time for my work, has been a battle from the beginning.

Wanting to have it all has meant that I have sometimes come unstuck. In 1978, I gave birth to my second child and six months later held my first solo exhibition at the Ewing and George Paton Galleries at Melbourne University. My then husband and I drove to Melbourne from the country and left the children with their grandparents, before heading to the opening. As there were no mobile phones, I had no idea that baby Will screamed in agony until his eardrum burst.

Family and work have always been in competition for me. There is urgency and pleasure in both, but not at the same time. Perhaps grandmothering will mend this division within me? Grandmothering is simpler and takes me backwards and forwards in time in a lovely way. Age has given me perspective, which means I am puzzled at some of the things my younger self did in terms of my divided loyalties.

Now I am involved and able to help in practical ways. It is all familiar and all new. I needed to be reminded how to change nappies and how to make up a bottle. I had to learn how to stuff Penelope into onesies and her sleeping bag, because neither item was around when I had my children. Something about Penelope's routine, established early by Bella, her mother, focuses and slows me down. It also reminds me of being a young mother with energy. And ignorance.

Penelope is an easy baby who likes her sleep. But I'm constantly impressed how, once in her sleeping bag, thumb in her mouth, bundled up with a soft toy, she is off to sleep without a squawk. When I stay the night, I can pick her up if she wakes and snuggle into her warm smell. When she's awake, she can now look me straight in the eye, look at me and then look away, taking everything in. To my daughter Harriet, I remark how self-absorbed Penelope is. She disagrees: 'Look at her looking at everything.' Penelope is both self-absorbed and extroverted. She is already a person, already complex.

I laugh every time I watch the video of Penelope tasting a lemon and gagging, just like an adult. In a painterly photograph of Penelope at daycare, she has crawled into a basket and fallen asleep, the sun on her cheek, her thumb in her mouth, surrounded by a soft toy, an open book, green grass and a red truck. When she began crawling, she would take off, head down. Months later, I witnessed her evident pleasure in standing upright. Her mother sent me a video of her on a sunny morning in the laundry: Penelope pushes a trolley of blocks into a pile of dirty washing, takes the coloured blocks out one at a time, bangs them together, places the blue ones to left, the yellow ones to the right, then puts them all back in the trolley. Wanting a further adventure, she climbs over the blocks and through the handles of the trolley as if in an obstacle race.

I study a video of Lucky, asleep in Ibiza, dreaming of sucking, an Australian football game on the television in the background. Lucky was born during a hot Spanish summer. Sometimes he wears a nappy, never much else. I watch him lying on a sheepskin, cooing enchantingly; it is a Manet-like scene of sunshine, his mother and Will picnicking with friends by a river. The end of the video is punctuated by Lucky having a poo, no nappy. Not Manet.

I try to remember our family at these young stages. My parents married in England and left for Australia in 1948. My father said to his twenty-four-year-old wife, 'Take a good look at your parents as you will never see them again.' And she didn't. I was born in the Mercy Hospital, Melbourne, with two horns on my head, so I was rushed away into a humidicrib. No one told my mother what was happening. A wreath arrived and she assumed it was for her newborn, two-horned baby. In fact, it was for her mother, who had died the day I was born. Once again, another death, another birth.

I have only hazy memories of my other grandparents. My father's mother died when I was four. I was told that she doted on me, but I can't remember her. Perhaps this explains why my pleasure in grandmothering has been such a surprise to me.

My husband's mother, Dorothy, was eighty-eight when we took Harriet, the last of her twelve grandchildren, to meet her. Between Harriet and Dorothy, the life span stretched back to Dorothy having her tonsils removed without anaesthetic in 1905. What will Penelope and Lucky find amazing about me and my life when they look back like this?

My mother has been the memorable grandparent for my children. Or perhaps I should say, the model for haphazard, if loving, grandparenting? There and not there. Charlie remembers his grandmother collecting him from school, riding the clutch and skidding in the tram tracks. He also remembers her serving crème caramel for dessert. Less rosy is his memory of her when she moved in to mind the three of them while we were away. One night, she woke him when she was having an asthma attack. Terrified, he held her mask to her face so she could breathe, and drove her across a busy main road, back to her house. At sixteen, he knew how to drive, but had no licence. When Harriet was a teenager, she locked herself out of our apartment and had to catch the tram to Grandma's house. She found her seventy-eight-year-old grandmother standing on the dining-room table, trying to change a light bulb. While loving and wanting to hold onto the baby stages of my grand-children, I look back on those interactions between my mother and her grandchildren and I envisage different future pleas-ures for myself as my grandchildren grow up.

Having arrived at this stage in life, I also see the past in a new light. Despite never changing a nappy, my first husband's mother was a terrific grandmother. She remained an involved and positive force in her grandsons' lives even after our divorce took them far from the next paddock, where we had lived. Until now, I had no idea how painful that change must have been for her. She visited us, and rang regularly to talk to them, and to me about them.

Thirty-four years ago, when I was pregnant with Harriet, Jim and I made a trip to New York to look at art. I was on the lookout for paintings of babies that had meaning for me, not just 'Madonna and Child' paintings, in which most of the babies look like miniature men. Now I have even more reason to be on the lookout for baby paintings. I realise that, all those years ago, I was searching for a tradition to work within. I am still searching, perhaps with more urgency.

While I am interested in women who painted babies and in those who managed to both work and be mothers, one of my favourite paintings of a baby is by Van Gogh. Through the energy and turbulence in his use of paint in *Madame Augustine Roulin and Baby Marcelle*, he gives us a real baby, one who engages with the viewer, one we might see on the street, who might make eye contact with us. Yet, despite the ordinary setting, Van Gogh's mother and baby arrangement is still a variation on the 'Madonna and Child' pose, the thick yellow paint behind the baby suggesting an eternal halo. A picture painted by a man who never had a child. Perhaps this explains its power.

The great American portrait artist Alice Neel (1900–1984), whose subjects were her relatives, friends and neighbours, is one of very few artists to paint her grandchildren. Her portrait *Mother and Child (Nancy and Olivia)* reads as a contemporary 'Madonna and Child', although Nancy and Olivia are not at all generalised figures, but are painted with startling, if disturbing, precision and particularity. There is, as in many of Neel's portraits, an aura of anxiety about the subjects. In her 1934 nude painting of her six-year-old daughter Isabetta, the girl stands facing the viewer, strong, confronting. Isabetta was raised by her Cuban grandparents. Neel saw her again only twice, and repainted the portrait in 1935. I find myself reacting emotionally to the powerful work and difficult life of Alice Neel, and of the German painter Paula Modersohn-Becker. Both were modernist in style, but chose the deeply personal, female subjects of pregnancy, babies and children, subjects that had traditionally been considered insignificant. While Neel led a long and tough life, Modersohn-Becker died at only thirty-two, ten days after giving birth to her only child.

It is not that artists don't choose to paint babies and children—they do. The paintings, however, rarely feature in catalogues or retrospectives, as, until recently, they have been considered minor works—the central miracle of life relegated to the margins. The issue has been compounded by the historical invisibility of women artists. But things are changing. The writer and art critic Jennifer Higgie has for many years posted a woman artist's work and biography on Instagram every day. Now we can see, digitally, more paintings by women, and more in which babies, children, grandchildren and mothers are subjects. How exhilarating it is that these subjects are emerging from the shadows of the 'domestic' and 'minor'.

I look forward to my grandchildren drawing and painting with me. Will I paint my grandchildren? It's early days, but so far I choose to use my iPhone to document them. Drawing and painting them would involve my interpretation and that's not what I'm after at the moment. But virtual or painted records are nothing compared to holding a baby in your arms, laughing with them—and being the subject of that all powerful gaze.

Carol Raye

From Ballerina to Grandmother

My beautiful granddaughter Charlotte, who is twenty-six, goes into my wardrobe and sighs with pleasure. My clothes are wonderful, she tells me, the most wonderful vintage. Vintage? Really? To me they are just my clothes, lovely clothes, but just what I wear. They speak of me. I don't feel vintage.

I have been a grandmother since I was seventy. I am now ninety-seven and I can honestly say that not only have I learned a lot, but I have had the joyous experience of watching another generation of our family grow up. And this has been a totally different experience from that of watching my own children grow up. The times we live in are different now, but I am also a very different person from who I was at twenty-eight, when our first baby was born.

During a successful career as a ballerina and top-billing

theatre and film actress in England, I had fallen in love with a young, newly qualified veterinary surgeon, Robert Ayre-Smith. He went on to pursue a degree in agriculture at Cambridge and was awarded a Fulbright scholarship to the University of Louisiana. It was there, in Baton Rouge, that we were married, in 1951, during those hopeful post-war years.

The following year we returned to England, where our first daughter, Sally Jane, was born. Sally was only three months old when we set off to Kenya, where Robert had been appointed by the Colonial Veterinary Service to run a 10,000-acre government experimental farm in the Rift Valley. Our son Mark was born in 1953, and a few years later we had another daughter, Harriet. I'm happy to say our three children are still with us and we have, in addition, three grandchildren, Finn, Charlotte and Indie, now aged twenty-seven, twenty-six and twenty-four.

In 1964, we sailed on the *Oriana* to Sydney, where Robert joined the CSIRO as a principal research scientist. We settled into our new life in Australia and I returned to my career by joining Channel 7 as a TV producer. At the time, it was an uncommon occupation for a woman. Life was full with children and work. Later, when Robert went to work in Baghdad, Spain and Honduras, the children and I went to live with my parents in England and we joined Robert for holidays. It was an unusual way to live and eventually we all decided that we missed Australia and would like to return and make a permanent home here.

Mark and his family live in Far North Queensland. Sally

Jane pursued a successful career as a producer in film and television, is married, but has no children. Harriet is married and has a daughter. Her husband is Australian, but they live and work in America. So I have not been able to see my grandchildren as consistently as I would have liked to. Nevertheless, the gaps between our meetings have, in certain ways, enhanced our relationships. I was lucky to get to know them well when they were young, so our emotional closeness remains strong, despite the physical distance between us. As they have grown up, their individual characters have developed, which is a wonderful experience for a grandmother to witness.

Their world is unimaginably different from the one in which I grew up, in England. I didn't know my mother's parents at all. Her father died before I was born and her mother died when I was just one or two, so my paternal grandparents were the only grandparents I had. And they played an important part in my life.

My grandmother was a very strong woman. She went to work when she was still a child, because they were poor, there were lots of brothers and sisters, and their father had died. I remember her telling me the sweet story of when she went to a clothing factory to see if she could get a job, because she could sew. In those days you couldn't get ready-made clothing—everything was handmade. The foreman said to her, 'How old are you?' She replied, 'Eleven.' He then asked her to spell 'work' and she said, 'W-o-r-k.' Then he asked her to spell 'walk'. When she hesitated, he said, 'Look, come back later. I think you should do a bit more schooling.' She did go back, and she worked hard all her life.

I remember her stories of taking in lodgers: she was determined to earn extra money so that her three children would have a proper education and a much better way of life than her own early years. And this she achieved. My father had a successful career in the Royal Navy and his brother and sister had executive positions in the civil service.

My grandmother was the dominant person in their marriage; my grandfather was gentle and clever, and told me lovely stories. He spent most of his working life in the Thames Water Police. I still have his large metal police whistle, which I carry in my handbag.

My grandmother, that little girl who asked to work in the factory, was a very fine seamstress. One of my treats when I was little was to be allowed to look at the marvellous boxes of Victorian buttons in her sewing cupboard. Some of those glorious buttons and trimming would now be very valuable. Another memory: when I was quite small and feeling cold at bedtime, my grandmother would warm newspaper in front of the fire and wrap it round my bare feet. 'There's nothing like warm newspaper to warm you,' she'd say. Nowadays, with electric blankets, that sounds a bit ridiculous, but at the time it was gorgeous.

She also had a wonderful, long gold muff chain, on the end of which was a gold pocket watch. Every dress she wore had a little pocket for it. When she died, she left the chain to me and the watch to my cousin. We both treasure these items.

My grandmother was not a tall woman, about

five-foot- two, but she held herself upright and was strong. Most of the photos of her as a young woman were taken in the age when subjects had to pose and keep still when a camera was pointed at them, so people often look somewhat severe. Photographs can lie. My grandmother was a smiling person, warm and kind, attractive, as was my grandfather. I always thought of them as caring people, never intimidating, and I always looked forward to seeing them. That says a lot. My grandmother always smelled beautiful and it was such a pleasure in my life to be with her, and with my grandfather.

They had always lived in London, but when the war came their area was badly bombed and my father brought them to live with us, just outside Portsmouth, at Binfield in Hampshire. By the time the war ended, it seemed unsuitable for them to return to London, so my father built a granny flat and they lived with us until they died at an old age. My parents also came to live with me in their later life. I think that is what family is all about, being together, looking after each other.

My grandparents had a big influence on my life as a young girl. Life with them and my parents was secure, filled with the certainties of love and belonging. In contrast, my grandchildren's world is global, and seems to me to be full of uncertainties. My relationship with them is, therefore, different from my grandparents' relationship with me.

I found it easy being a new grandmother. The joy and wonder that I still feel at the birth of a new, tiny human must be universal. A baby grandchild who needs looking after evokes similar feelings as one's own children did as babies. But as a grandmother, I had a lot more time than I did as a mother, and I could enjoy and indulge, without having the full responsibility of parenthood—without those feelings of guilt at never being good enough. And then, of course, there is the other side of the coin in the new relationship, that of the child's perception of the grandparent.

Watching the English 2019 D-day Remembrance commemorations on television with my grandchildren was a strange experience. As my father was in the navy, I grew up in Portsmouth, where the ceremonies took place, and where D-day was launched from. As it happened, I was visiting my parents from London for a few days and I noticed that both sides of the lane in front of my parents' house were filled with army vehicles, nose to tail—a most unusual sight. We had no idea what was going on; as it was wartime, we just assumed it was an exercise of some sort. Watching the re-enactment on TV of that huge moment in history seventy-five years later, with my grandchildren, I could say to them that I was not only alive back then, but actually there, physically—things like that are so radically different from the things I shared with my grandparents. My grandchildren know I was there, but what does this momentous event mean to them?

I like to think of my role as a grandparent as a special privilege, because a grandmother can give a unique feeling of security in today's world, which seems so volatile and invasive for young people, especially when they are confronted by 24/7 media. Providing that extra feeling of stability, as someone who has lived through significant moments in history—been there, really, on D-day—and still survived and is part of your family and loves you—this is a true grandparent's role, and a most gratifying one. I am still here, so I give my grandchildren an intimate sense of continuity, a thread to their own past.

Of my three grandchildren, it is Charlotte whom I have seen the most, because she was born in Sydney and I often looked after her when she was little. I have vivid memories of taking her for walks in her pram, visiting the antiques market and pointing out things to this two-year-old who was genuinely curious about the various objects. A few years later, I was teaching her to sew and knit. It was lovely to see her joy and excitement when she found out how to thread a sewing needle, use a thimble and knit a little scarf for her favourite doll. I think of my grandmother and her nimble fingers and I choose to believe that this direct line between us later came in useful for Charlotte at Oxford University, when she was directing and producing plays and was able also to design and make the costumes for her actors.

I also loved teaching her to make pastry for the family mince pies that I always made at Christmas time. I'm thrilled to say she still makes them today!

Another and different occasion was her first proper haircut. I took her to my own hairdresser's, where I had been a client for many years. Before he put the cotton smock on her, John sat her on my knee in front of the mirrors, in case she was intimidated in any way. Instead, she just clung to me and said, 'It's all right, Grannyma, don't be scared. It'll be all right.'

At all of two and a half, she was looking after me!

A more recent memory, and one I cherish, is when Charlotte came home from Oxford to speak at my darling husband Robert's memorial service in Sydney in 2016. She spoke movingly of her relationship with her grandfather:

> *When I was thirteen, my grandfather sent me a book in the post that changed my life—or rather, because I was only thirteen, made my life what it has become. I'm sure he did not intend for it to have the effect it did. It was an innocuous paperback, maroon, with a small picture on the cover of a man with close-cropped hair, sitting in front of an uneaten dinner with a wine bottle at his elbow. An image curiously unrelated to the content of the book itself, because the book was Turgenev's* Fathers and Sons. *I had never read anything so serious, and my thirteen-year-old eyes were burning with tears of awe and reverence. That was the beginning of my impassioned relationship with Russian literature.*
>
> *A year later I found myself spending a week or two in Robert and Carol's flat in Woollahra and I could not sleep most nights for jetlag mingled with a vein of homesickness. And during those long nights I read* War and Peace *and* Anna Karenina. *Sometimes I would bring my books to the breakfast table in the morning, and Robert would take them and hum in approbation. He told me that it had*

taken him several months to read War and Peace, *which made me feel better about the difficulties I was having. He apparently read it on a boat to Brazil. So it was that Robert opened an entire world at my feet, which I have been exploring to the best of my ability.*

I think this illustrates what an influence grandparents can have on grandchildren, grandfathers as well as grandmothers.

Charlotte says that Robert taught her how to be at ease, no matter where she found herself. He taught her that thinking, just thinking, is a glorious thing to do. Subsequently, whenever she is under pressure, she says to herself, *No, stop it, Robert would not approve.* Robert also loved music. One of his favourite pieces was Schubert's 'Ava Maria', and whenever the world crowds in on Charlotte or she feels lonely, she will play this song and remember the things her grandfather taught her.

My two grandsons are not as familiar to me now as they were when they were younger. When they moved to Sydney, they would drop in after school and partake of my cooking and enjoy discussing their schoolwork with Robert. They have both grown into attractive young men, different from one another in personality and temperament, but with a family similarity. Finn, the elder, is thoughtful, sensitive and developing a love for his home in Far North Queensland. Indie is gregarious and enjoying studying at the Film and Television School.

I have come to the conclusion that the contribution of grandparents to family life, while not a necessity, is certainly an asset. This was brought home to me recently, when the young daughter of friends of my daughter Sally Jane, whose farm I live on, asked Sally if she would be a de facto grandmother at her school on Grandmother Day, because her real grandparents were in South Africa, where she used to live. My daughter accepted instantly, having realised how upset her young friend would be on the day, not to have a grandmother of her own like everyone else. It was apparently a very happy occasion for all.

Being a grandparent is not only a privilege and a joy, but also a challenge in today's world, and doubly so if one is as old as I am. But, without wanting to be greedy, I wonder if I will live long enough to have the added joy of being a great-grandmother! Great-grandmother to a girl, perhaps, who would also appreciate my clothes, vintage or not.

Cheryl Kernot

The Face at the Cat Flap

I had the unusual opportunity of a practice run at being a grandparent. When I was living in London in 2006, one of my adult students, Olivia, Ugandan by birth, chose me to be her 'adopted' mother. Back in Kampala, she had been a street child, staying in a lean-to church refuge. A Lutheran priest there had recognised her abilities and sponsored her education right through to university. He died just before she graduated. She did not know where her mother was.

Olivia won a scholarship to the School for Social Entrepreneurs in London, where I was the director of teaching and learning in the first few years of my post-political life. She founded and ran a small not-for-profit in East London. I came to admire her tenacity, optimism and commitment to making life better for the children of African parents with

HIV/AIDS in East London. One of the services she designed was for volunteers to visit their homes to help with meals and homework, to keep the children living a home routine and attending school as regularly as possible.

The two of us clicked. Olivia involved me in her work and invited me to her home for huge Ugandan meals. I've definitely had more than my share of green banana, goat meat and pan-fried flatbreads. A year after completing her studies, she asked me to be her birth partner. I felt a sense of panic, which only increased as the due date approached. But, as it turned out, it was a bonus that I was there to intervene after three days of intermittent labour. 'And who are you?' asked the bossy midwife. 'My mother,' said Olivia. 'Stepmother,' said her Ugandan partner. After another twelve hours of induction overnight and an emergency caesarean just before the morning change of shift, I was the only one left standing to welcome into the world the shrivelled little human, to be named Gavin. I tried to speak in a soothing voice; I dressed him and made sure he got something to drink. I felt as if we bonded there and then. I stayed with Gavin and his parents in their home for the first two weeks, then visited every second day. Needless to say, we were all much better prepared for the birth of his brother David a little more than a year later, when I was once again the birth partner.

We remain very close to this day, even if we have only communicated via Skype during these past four years since they returned to Uganda and then back to London. The many photographs I have of them as babies and toddlers, the outings

I took them on because their parents couldn't afford to, all of that has become an important part of our shared family folklore. This year I sent them money for a trip to the movies, including treats to eat, an indulgence beyond their current family budget.

In 2012, the news that I was to become an actual blood grandmother caught me by surprise. I had a busy academic life in Sydney, punctuated by spots of political commentary. My daughter, twenty-eight, had been with her partner for six years and they had married in late December 2010. I had presumed the usual marriage–house–child timeline would be followed. So when I was emailed a photo of a scan, I had to look closely several times before I could join the dots. I was completely unprepared. Especially in my head, I was not ready. I hadn't allowed my thoughts to wander there. So I disappointed them immediately by saying, 'Really?' My first selfish thoughts were: 'How will I fit this into my busy life? How can I find emotional space for this in my head?' Those of us who've had a child often say 'wait and see how you feel' to new parents who insist they'll be going back to work soon after giving birth. I needed to take my own advice: I too needed to wait and see.

My daughter was quite ill for the first several months of the pregnancy, so all attention was focused on helping her to cope and to continue working. I was invited to attend various scans but didn't. It was their baby, not mine. Despite my daughter saying I should feel free to be involved only as much as I wanted to be, I did feel just a little pressure to participate more in the pregnancy. I was happy, though, to accompany her and support her for non-standard appointments, such as a cervical 'sweep' for overdue babies—a painful experience for my daughter.

I had the whooping-cough vaccinations now required by those planning to be in contact with newborns, and thought about what I might choose to be called as a grandmother, if I weren't already given a unique name by my grandchild. Despite researching various cultural alternatives, I settled on *Nanna*, after my own, who was very warm and loving. I also instinctively chose a teddy bear as a birth present and it has been that grandchild's favourite sleeping companion for the last seven years.

Throughout the pregnancy, I consciously paid more attention to friends and family who had been grandparents for a while. I observed two trends: firstly, the expectation that grandma/grandpa would be very available to babysit while parents worked, and secondly, that one could easily morph into being a grandparent first and foremost, at the expense of one's previous persona. I particularly didn't want the latter to happen to me. There would be no brag books proffered without invitation, no constant references to my grandchild in conversations with others.

The length of my daughter's labour mirrored mine, and Toby was born at ten p.m—the same time his mother had been born! Having waited outside all day, I was shocked at my son-in-law's first words to me when he emerged, beaming, from the birthing suite: 'Mum, he's got your nose!' A face palm emoji would adequately capture my response. I hadn't quite realised at the time just how significant this nose business was for him—he is Samoan and was expecting to see a flat nose on his son. Toby's nose looked pretty flat to me. I could see only his paternal grandfather looking back at me. How amazing, then, that Toby and I do indeed now share a nose shape and even the occasional simultaneous nose bleed.

In the days following his birth, he didn't sleep much, didn't cry either, just kept his bright little eyes open wide, taking in the sounds and lights of the world around him. Over the coming months, like most grandparents, I couldn't see enough of him. I melted in adoration, along with his parents, at all his milestones: the eyes looking straight back at you, the first smile, the 'language' and all the rest. And he has me to thank for recognising his growing appetite and moving him onto solids sooner than his mother had planned. The moment he took my hand in his to guide his first spoonful of cereal into his mouth, then reached hungrily for more, is a powerful memory for me and his parents.

I continued to work full-time and added 'Nanna Time' to my list of things to fit into my life.

My uncle and my father often told me how much I reminded them of my maternal grandfather—not physically, but because of my interest in politics and talking about politics from a very young age. As a child, I wasn't aware that my grandfather was asked to be a political candidate for Labor in a Hunter Valley coalfields seat in the late 1940s. He decided that he preferred to run campaigns instead, which he did successfully for a decade. I am the only one of his six grand-children to have inherited that interest. He died when I was just eleven and I regret now that I never got to have an adult political conversation with him, and that he didn't get to see my election to parliament.

Imagine how my attention was piqued when, at age four, Toby turned the pages of the newspaper and proceeded to ask a few questions about what he could see. Then, at six, he looked up from whatever he was doing and asked me to explain the 'breaking news' story on the news channel. Simplifying international events and describing Donald Trump was a challenge, and often the chance for a bit of fun. But did my genes play any role in his success in the public-speaking contest in kindergarten and then in Grade One? And in the fact that he really likes doing it? I can only smile, enjoy his enjoyment of it and hope to explain, over time, concepts like fairness and justice and equality, in ways that might matter to his young life. I had no success in talking him out of choosing Godzilla as his 'A day in the life of...' project. But what would I know? He won the school event (beating children in a class above him) because he knew his subject and was able to speak and engage with enthusiasm.

Once a week, my neighbour (who has no children) and I go to the delightful little public school nearby, to help with reading in Toby's class. There are grandparents' afternoon teas and special assemblies to attend—I even fill in for my daughter at Parents' and Citizens' meetings when she can't attend. I'm also enrolled in training to become an ethics teacher. I have come to realise how much Toby enjoys my involvement in his school life, and it reminds me that I wasn't able to do as much for my daughter when she was at school at his age. Thank goodness I have replaced that previous clutter of city life with a clearer mind and deeper thinking, and have made myself more available!

Several factors—the cost of housing in Sydney, the need for my daughter to revert to part-time work when their child was born, as well as my wanting to downscale my work responsibilities—all led to our joint decision to move to the Hunter Valley, where I was born and grew up and where my daughter spent many happy school holidays with her maternal grandparents and cousins. We were going to pool our resources and design our own version of intergenerational living.

First we had to find a house with the right skeleton for renovation. A backyard for children to play in was important. In the process of house-hunting, we were astonished to discover just how many big old backyards had been subdivided—to make a buck, no doubt. Eventually, we found the right one to renovate so that we had a single common wall that had a secure locked door, two small decks for me, two large common decks, and space for me well beyond the standard granny-flat specifications. As we had already shared a two-bedroom unit for a few months prior to moving, the challenges of living together during the renovations seemed minor.

Shared rituals of childhood are important. My sister and I still talk of things we did together, particularly catching the (steam) train to stay the weekend with Nanna and Pop. I may be only on the other side of the hard-to-keep-locked door if I'm needed, but on most Saturdays, Toby and I celebrate 'Nanna Night'. He comes over to sleep in my bed and we play cards, read, watch a movie or even play the dreaded *Minecraft* together on our individual screens. I am not very good at it and he patiently takes my screen and catches me up with the action. In the morning we have 'French Breakfast': croissants and hot chocolate with a marshmallow or two on top.

Toby had our undivided love and attention until, when he was almost five, little Isobel was born. It reminded me of when I was at a prenatal class, preparing for the birth of my first child, and the instructor told those expecting their second child that, even though they were wondering if they could love a second one as much as their first, it would take just one look to fall in love all over again. As it was for me with my grand-children.

Isobel's impending arrival was announced to me via Toby's T-shirt: *I'm an only child…until February.* Her birth was swift and natural. Toby (who had wanted to be present) and I arrived about an hour afterwards. When Toby was born, a carload of excited rellies, including his great-grand-mother, made a two-hour trip down to the Sydney hospital, arriving by nine a.m. the next morning. This time we all left the local hospital within six hours of the birth and gathered at Isobel's great-grandmother's house, so the new baby could meet her extended maternal family. My mother is ninety-seven and delighted to be around to meet her newest great-grandchildren. Toby is particularly close to her and has enjoyed her teaching him to play card games, especially Strip Jack Naked, which was so useful for his developing maths skills. It seemed right for us all to celebrate Isobel's birth with my mother, and it was an especially lovely time.

We're quite a matriarchal family, so raising an active, single-minded boy had been a new challenge. Isobel would be more familiar, we thought.

Two years and four months later, Izzy and I have developed our own rituals born of her interests. We tour the garden looking for ripe strawberries to pick and eat; we lie on the grass looking up at the sky and describe what we can see; she raids the drawer of my bedside table. On the mornings when she leaves for preschool she calls out, 'Bye, Nanna. Have a day!'

Intergenerational living that allows for separate spaces is a distinctly twenty-first-century evolution. In the past, many couples who, of necessity, started out living with their parents never had private space for themselves. How has this version worked for me? Most of my friends say they couldn't and wouldn't want to do it. My nieces say they couldn't do it. It definitely has its moments. My daughter has developed her 'Back off, Mum!' response for the bigger issues. Disagreements with a son-in-law are more complex. Fortunately, there aren't many of those. He has told others that he thinks it's a positive for his children that I am there.

I had naively expected to be able to maintain similar levels of privacy, space and time for reading and watching my favourite television programs as I had had before we moved in 'together'. Not so. The lockable door handle on the common door has had to be reinforced, but Isobel, especially, is quick as lightning to get out of her back door and across to mine whenever she feels a deliberate barrier has been placed in her way. Toby can usually find the key.

But who could ignore a little face at the raised flap of the cat door, calling 'Nanna!', when, on nights her family has gone to bed early, this two-year-old has negotiated the hallway on her side, in darkness? Not me. Such things are precious memories. And anyway, before you know it, grandchildren are at school, gone during the day.

In some ways, I feel as if I'm reliving aspects of parenthood: always picking up children's clothes and toys left on the floor, sweeping up ever-present crumbs, sharing a shower. Once a week, I cook a meal, a roast or osso bucco, or a hearty winter stew, and they visit 'Nanna's house' to eat dinner together. We started out eating most meals together, but I now prefer a quieter ambience, so to speak. I come and go, with some travel and the occasional teaching day or two. Homecomings are still greeted with excitement and hugs. And, maybe, a treat from me.

So, five years on, apart from my proximity to what my doctor describes as a 'perfect germ factory' and thus more viruses than ever in my life, the trade-offs have been worth it. I am already there on birthdays and for Xmas. And, as I am present in so much of my grandchildren's lives, I can also witness all the important little things. Yes, I'm often called on to babysit, but no more so than in most families, I suspect.

Because I am already there, they sometimes come into my bed early in the morning for snuggles, and we can have a spontaneous swim at the beach, or I can help with homework.

Best of all, though, is when they draw pictures of their family and there's always a smiling Nanna.

Mona Mobarek

The Dearest Child is the Child of Your Child

This piece of writing is dedicated to the light of my life, my beautiful three-year-old grandchild Faatima. After I'm gone, she will have a piece of me to carry with her all her life, and I hope she will understand through my words the depth of my love for her and the importance of a grandmother in one's life. My legacy to her is simply love.

I am also dedicating this piece to my paternal grandmother, Qadria Leila. Her name in Arabic has a few shades of meaning: the one who is capable, who embodies honour, dignity, power, endurance and greatness. She was an extraordinary and loving woman who taught me how to express love wholeheartedly. She shaped me and shaped the grandmother I have become, the grandmother I am. For this I am truly grateful and will always hold her in high esteem and deep affection.

I discovered why we are called grandmothers when Faatima was born: we have so much to offer this new generation of family; life becomes grand after the entry of a new little one into our world. And life has become even grander, as we have been blessed with another grandchild, Muhammad Lateef, an adorable, happy baby boy, now five months old, whose smile has me weak at the knees. When I first saw him, I was transported back to the birth of my own baby boy Adam, his father, thirty years ago. My two grandchildren are the centre of my world and I cannot wait to share the same connection with Muhammad as I have with Faatima. I secretly hope that their parents are always busy, so I have an excuse to spend more time looking after them.

Faatima arrived at a very painful time in our life. We received the news that we were going to be grandparents about a month after we lost our youngest daughter, our beloved Sara, to Hodgkin's lymphoma. She was only twenty-one. Her death shook me to the core as a mother. My heart shattered and I wondered whether I would ever mend and whether the tightness in my chest would ever subside. The news that I was going to be a grandmother could not have come at a more perfect time. I could face life again. I felt I had something to live for and to look forward to. Faatima's entry into the world began a new chapter in my life, one filled with hope and joy.

My son rang at two o'clock in the morning on the fourteenth of March 2016 with the news that we had a healthy baby girl, born at her home in the eastern suburbs of Melbourne. My excited husband rushed to our bedroom and whispered to me: 'Wake up, Nena, your granddaughter has arrived.' You would have thought I was twenty again from the speed with which I leapt out of bed and got dressed. We arrived without breaking the speed limit. Once I had congratulated the new parents, I got down to the real reason for being there at such an ungodly hour.

As soon as I saw her, I was filled with an overwhelming sense of love and pure joy. She was a rather small baby with olive skin and thick, dark-brown hair. She also had the longest eyelashes and most defined eyebrows I have ever seen. A perfect specimen of creation. Tears welled in my husband's eyes and in that moment we both knew that this child was now the centre of our world. Being from an Arab background, we tend to ignore personal space and privacy, so we were at the house every single day for six weeks, showering the household with food and gifts for the baby. We eventually eased off and visited every second day. It was like a drug of addiction. We had to have our fix otherwise we would go into withdrawal.

The depth of my connection with Faatima was and is clear for all to see. Our bond began as early as three months for her, when her eyes followed me wherever I went. For me, it began the moment I saw her. There are so many priceless moments we have shared with Faatima, but one of my favourites is when she was about eight months old and she came to visit with her parents. Apparently, this clever little girl knew exactly where she was when she arrived at our front door. She started flapping her arms and legs and making noises, as if to say, 'Hurry up and open the door so I can see my grandma.' When she saw me, she gave me a huge smile and threw herself on me. It was such a heart-melting moment, captured by my son on his phone. I can't tell you how many times I have watched that video.

As Faatima grew, so did our bond. I took care of her quite regularly as her mother was involved in Islamic community work. She is a participant in the interfaith program and takes tours to a range of mosques in Melbourne. Faatima's father is a Sunday-school teacher. He teaches Islamic History, the Quran and Basic Arabic. My son is following my lead: I used to teach Islamic Studies to children in the south-eastern suburbs of Melbourne, and later taught teenagers at the Heidelberg Mosque. Faatima's maternal grandparents are prominent members of the Islamic community and have served the wider community through various interfaith programs. Faatima is fortunate to have all her family members in agreement about her Islamic upbringing. We all want her to learn and appreciate her heritage and rich cultural background. We also want her to live in peace and harmony in this country.

Faatima has always loved coming to our house. Perhaps she understands that this is the house where 'Yes, sweetheart' are the words she will always hear. I occasionally say no, but when she looks at me with those pleading eyes, well, it is obvious what usually happens.

My daughter, now thirty-two, often remarks on how much Faatima gets away with. She says my parenting style has softened. 'But I'm not her parent,' I respond. 'I'm her grandparent, which entitles me to spoil her as I see fit.' I guess I now know why my mum used to make hot chips for my kids at eleven o'clock at night on demand.

My mother's indulgence of my children used to horrify me, yet I find myself at the stove at midnight making popcorn for Faatima. It is no surprise that, when she leaves our house, she is kicking and screaming. Despite being exhausted, I feel she has taken a part of me with her. I long for the moment I will see her again.

I have always loved children, loved being with them, and I have set up a room in our house especially for Faatima. It is full of toys, dolls, books, puzzles and all sorts of activities. We also have a big cinema screen for her to enjoy her favourite shows. She knew what Netflix was before she was two years old and would often say 'Netblix'.

This is a far cry from my own childhood, when my sister and I entertained ourselves for hours picking up stones in the garden and playing Jacks. Some might say Faatima is being spoilt rotten, but I say I am creating an environment that she never wants to leave. It is her little haven, her retreat, and she knows it. Children are intuitive beings and know who goes the extra mile for them; that is why Faatima is so attached to me. When she is at our house, she is quite disengaged from everyone else. Only Nena is allowed to do things for her. My poor husband occasionally sneaks off to visit her in her own home, so he can have time with her, without me.

I was excited to take Faatima to the Royal Melbourne

Show by myself this year. I had never taken my children on my own. We even took the train to make it into a little adventure. After some interesting and entertaining conversation, we finally arrived and Faatima's first comment was: 'Nena, where is the show?' I replied: 'Sweetheart, this is the show.' She stared at me, a confused look in her eyes, but quickly settled after the purchase of her first showbag. We did all the usual show activities, but within an hour she wanted to go home. I was shocked! What child wants to leave the show after such a short time? Faatima. She preferred to be at Nena's house. It was Tuesday, our special day together every week. What a wonderful feeling, knowing that your grandchild loves to spend time with you and enjoys being in your home so much that not even the show can compete.

I now understand the old Egyptian saying: *The dearest child is the child of your child*. I used to think this was ridiculous. How can you love any child more than your own? Impossible! Any mother knows this. Now I laugh at my short-sightedness. I have come to understand and embrace this wisdom. As I have matured in years, I have seen the world through different lenses and know now that a grandchild is the most precious child to touch your heart and life. It is your own child twice over.

Where do we learn to be grandmothers? Is it instinctive or do we have role models? A combination of both, I suspect. I was blessed in having an incredible role model in my paternal grandmother, Qadria Leila, who passed away when I was pregnant with Sara. She, like so many women of her time, was devoted to serving her family. Today she would be called a 'superwoman', but she was only doing what came naturally to her.

My grandmother had seven children of her own, plus the endless family members who constantly came to her house, usually seeking help and comfort. Things became even more hectic when my father married and brought his seventeen-year-old bride to live with his family. About two years later, I was born, then my sister sixteen months later. There were up to sixteen people living in the modest home. It may not have been big, but there was plenty of love and warmth.

My grandmother was a devout Muslim woman. She had a deep connection with her creator; serving her family and her husband's family was an expression of that connection. She was welcoming and never turned anyone away from her door. I was seven when I migrated with my parents and sister to Australia, but I still have powerful memories of my childhood in that house. There were five rooms that were used as bedrooms, a sitting room, a small formal lounge room, a small kitchen and one bathroom. Can you imagine how challenging it would be to share such limited space with so many people?

Who was Qadria Leila and what made her so special? She was born in 1916 in the town of Mansoura, approximately one hundred and fifty kilometres from Cairo. She was wise and worldly, despite her lack of formal education. She attended lessons at a local mosque, where she learnt to recite the Quran by heart. An attractive woman with a full figure, she dressed elegantly, especially when she went out. She loved colours; purple was her favourite. Lack of time and money meant she wore little jewellery and no make-up. Even though she was religious, she wasn't prudish and had a great sense of humour. Her talent for impersonating certain family members and neighbours provided the family with many moments of laughter. She had a strong personality and was not at all the submissive wife so common in her time.

My grandmother was special to me because, on top of her enormous responsibilities, she made time for me. I have fond memories of the cotton dolls she made me and the clothes she sewed for them. Where did she find the time? More importantly, how could she be bothered? Did she stay up late at night so she could surprise me in the morning with my new toy? I suspect she did.

Love shapes a child, and I have come to the realisation that I am a lot like my grandmother. I sew for Faatima as my grandmother sewed for me. I will always be in awe of Qadria Leila and her selflessness. Did she ever put herself first? I don't believe it would have occurred to her. She showed her love by serving others. Even when she had an opportunity to escape the whole clan to accompany her husband on a business trip, she took me with her.

Even after I married, she sat me on her lap and sang to me as if I was a little girl again. Such memories are etched in my heart. These are the feelings and memories that I would love my own grandchildren to have of me. Love like this is to be passed on from generation to generation.

My grandmother came to Australia twice. Once in 1974, when I was twelve, and again in 1988, when I was the mother of a one-year-old daughter, her first great-grandchild, Yasmeen. Both visits were exciting for me and the whole extended family. Qadria Leila spent most of her time caring for the children and making everyone's favourite dishes. Her trip was not a traditional holiday but rather another opportunity for her to serve her family. She gave and then looked to see what more she could give.

In 1991, my beloved grandmother became ill and was diagnosed with eye cancer. Being bedridden and looked after by others was devastating for her and she did not live long after her diagnosis. When she died, I remember thinking that life would never be the same for anyone who had experienced the warmth of her love. On my first trip back to Egypt after her death, I was heartbroken when I saw her empty home, which had always been full of people and activity. May she rest in eternal peace, and may I be half the grandmother that she was.

Love is the most precious gift that a grandmother can give. Her love, wisdom and experience connects her with her grandchildren in a special way. Those fortunate enough to have a loving and active grandmother in their life are blessed. Experiencing such love and connection is mutually beneficial. Many grandmothers have a renewed sense of purpose and a new focus in life. That is certainly the case for me: my grandchildren have restored my passion for life. I would love to live long enough to witness many more milestones in their lives.

Who knows? I may even sew Faatima's wedding dress. Maybe I'll be blessed enough to live this dream.

I must end here! Faatima has come bursting into the house, calling out, 'Nena? Nena? Nena?'

Joan London

How Do His Clear Eyes See Me?

Being a grandmother is rarely a role without precedents.

There was only one grandparent in my own childhood; all the others had died long before I was born. Grandma, my father's mother, occupied a special place in the family. Long widowed, she lived in a small, dark, one-storey, turn-of-the-century brick house in Mount Lawley, a respectable inner urban suburb of Perth. With her lived Dorrie, her eldest, childless daughter, and Jim, an ex-seaman from the north of England, whom Dorrie had married in her forties. Uncle Jim, a pipe-smoker, had a jolly face with fleshy jowls like a Toby jug and a voice so deep as to be almost indecipherable. His bed was on the back verandah, behind a partition—a 'sleep-out', as these spaces were called. Auntie Dorrie was known to be 'sensitive'—in fact, terribly touchy. She slept, with her hair in crisscrossed bobby pins, in the bedroom across the hall from her mother, to whom she was deeply attached. The line in the old song 'Billy Boy'—*She's a young thing and will not leave her mother*—always reminded me of my middle-aged Auntie Dorrie.

'Ma', as her children called my grandmother, was a quiet, dignified woman, an excellent cook and prodigious knitter, who knew how to hold her tongue and was deeply respected by her children and grandchildren. Long after her death, my father liked to quote her. He would preface his remarks with: 'My mother, a very wise woman, always used to say...'

A photograph of my grandmother's calm, thoughtful face hung on a wall in my parents' bedroom. 'Now, *there*,' said an interior decorator whom my mother once misguidedly consulted, 'is a woman of character.' During her brief visit to our house, these were the decorator's only words of praise.

We visited Grandma on Sunday afternoons. It was an occasion of clean clothes, washed face, tight plaits and, for me, a solid, greedy child ('such a plain little thing', I was mortified to overhear Auntie Dorrie say), the anticipation of cake and homemade lemon cordial, licorice allsorts and sugar-coated Aurora Jubes. Memories of the visit to Grandma in the early fifties now seem like a ritual set in Victorian times.

Because of her quietness and dignity, there was no doubt that the whole event centered on Grandma, even though she said very little, sitting in her chair, her knees covered with one of the rugs she had crocheted. In her presence, none of her grandchildren would dream of giggling or fighting. Even with my sister who was three years older than me, for whom I was the eternal enemy, we kept our spats down to a few hissed nudges and glares.

Grandma had been widowed during the Depression and all her four children had to find work, including my father, the youngest, who left school at fourteen and worked as an office boy to help support the family. My father often said he didn't know how his mother had managed in those years, and marvelled at her skills.

Grandma died when she was eighty-four. For some weeks after, my father was even quieter and more serious than usual. I don't remember feeling sorrow—Grandma was too distant, too old and quiet for that—but I've never forgotten her. She was a link to an older Australia. Born in the nineteenth century, a Victorian in her dress and manners, she was unforgettable in her poignant silence and self-possession.

•

My mother, Maisie, was five years old, with three younger brothers, when her mother died. Their father, an asthmatic, took off by himself to live in the north-west for his health, where he worked as a bookkeeper for a pearling firm in Broome. Who knows what adventures he had there? Decades later, my sisters and I were contacted by cousins we did not know existed.

Maisie went to live with her grandmother, also in Mount Lawley, and was later sent as a day student to Perth College, a private school for girls. Her three brothers, however, were brought up by a housekeeper in a distant part of the city. For the rest of her life she hardly knew them. Class—that bogey inherited from the English—came into it. It was a crippling legacy for my mother.

Whenever I asked my mother about her mother, she did not want to talk about her. It made her sad. She always spoke of her grandmother with deep respect. 'Gran was strict but very good to me,' she said. Her story reminded me of the many tales I had read about lively orphan girls sent to live with relatives—*Anne of Green Gables, Pollyanna, Seven Little Australians*—old-fashioned books that had been written in the late nineteenth or early twentieth century, which I inherited from my mother and older sisters. The loss of a mother, the orphan-hood of children, the role of grandparents in their upbringing were not uncommon stories then.

I remember lying in hospital, my newborn first child asleep in a bassinet beside my bed, and hearing the footsteps of my parents-in-law *running* up the corridor to my ward. My own parents, already grandparents nine times over, were more laid-back about the whole miracle, but this was the first grandchild for my parents-in-law. Immediately, my daughter was picked up, passed between them, family likenesses pronounced, As she was patted, rocked and spoken to, she lay very quiet, her eyes firmly closed. Soon, I knew, she would grow restless, bewildered, begin to cry, and I, still not at all sure about what to do, would be offered advice. I was beginning to learn that anyone who'd ever had a child was always ready and eager to give advice.

I have good memories of my mother in her role as grand-mother: she was easygoing, happy to be at home and surrounded by little children. She was named *Gan-gan* by her first grandchild, a title subsequently used by all her grand-children (and, she was pleased to find out, the name Queen Victoria was called by *her* grandchildren). I enjoyed watching my mother with my kids, how she loved simple things, being in the garden with them, or swimming in the ocean, and how often she would laugh with them at the antics of her ferocious little cat. Found as a kitten in the bush during our ill-con-ceived year of rural experiment, this cat was minded by my mother during our lengthy house renovations. She would hide and pounce on my mother's bridge-playing friends as they went to the toilet. When finally reunited with us in Fremantle, she disappeared forever into the city streets...

But there were times—there had always been times—when my mother would stay in bed, her head turned away from visitors to her room, the phone unplugged, not answer-able to the world. Sometimes I reflect on the anxiety that has manifested itself in different ways in all her daughters, as if there were some existential insecurity in our childhood that we have inherited.

By contrast, my mother-in-law was the children's *Nan*, a strong, contented and uncomplicated woman, and a wonderful cook. Our children looked forward to her sunny smile and her bountiful food. She had learned from her mother how to cook with confidence and to trust her intuition rather than books. Her generous meals burst with flavour. 'First, brown an onion,' she would intone.

She was my children's first experience of death. After visiting her in hospital and sensing she was about to die, my husband sped down the freeway to bring us back to say goodbye.

•

Now that first baby of mine has two children of her own, as does her brother. The four of them are aged between three and thirteen, and I have come to inhabit that curious grandparental emotion of instantly and deeply loving them, while being aware that I occupy a place of secondary importance. I think of us, the grandparents, as providing a sort of backup team, a well-meaning, cheerleading squad. Although we are never less than appreciative, I know that we are on the outer edge of the major drama, which is, of course, the relationship between children and their parents.

But there's relief too in the relinquishment of that huge responsibility, in knowing that you are not and will not be their final arbiters, or most potent influences, and of being able, as the cliché goes, to hand them back to their parents. We are on the sidelines now. As the oldest grandchild is about to turn fourteen, I'm also beginning to enjoy with her a new freedom in what I say; I can be honest, listen, put forward an opinion, or decide it would be wiser to hold my tongue. I remember when her mother was that age, and I watch my granddaughter repeating the hunger for clothes and the overwhelming focus on appearance.

Our grandchildren are moving further away, into their own lives, but those years of our involvement in their early childhood are what established the link that still exists, that I can only hope will always exist, in some form, between us. How to be secondary, how to watch and be called on if needed…As they become teenagers, we are less and less in their lives. Yet something lives on, maybe the greatest gift in a family: affection, and a deep, instinctive, almost humorous knowledge of each other. Our family holidays, when we all stay together in a large house down on the South Coast, expose us to one another with all our foibles, different temperaments and intimacies.

Grandchildren observe with such acuity, such direct sight. My husband installed some horizontal bars in the bedroom to allow him to hold yoga poses for his back. Our three-year-old grandson described the assembly of bars to me as 'that yoga thing that Buppi used to climb but now he puts his washing on it…'

I am a grandmother in modern form, in jeans and sneakers, aware when childminding of the importance of stimulation, initiating cooking projects, reading, drawing, acting games…anything to keep them from boredom and electronic devices. I know that now is the time to establish a relationship with them, before they are consumed by their own lives.

●

I have just come back from accompanying the youngest of my grandchildren, with his father, on a walk to the park, during which my three-year-old grandson, to the annoyance of my son, always protective of his mother, more than once affirmed that I was *old*: 'You are *old*, your hands are *old*.' How do his clear eyes see me? He is used to his parents and his aunts and uncles, and the assistants at his daycare, some of whom would be fifty years younger than I am. His grandparents must be the only members of the older generation in his life. I try to remember how I saw older female relatives when I was a child. As almost a different species, with their tight perms and corsets, large upholstered busts, bright-red lipstick and dabs of strong-smelling cologne behind the ears.

Perhaps that is one of the functions of a grandparent, to remind children of the ages of man. For them, we are the frontline representatives of what it means to be old. And, more than likely, in the future, it will be us who will furnish our grandchildren with their first experience of death.

Stephanie Alexander

With Love

I always wanted to be a grandmother, but was almost resigned to the fact that it was not going to happen for me.

My mother found that being a grandmother was a significant pleasure and she came to my rescue when I had a small baby and was trying to run a restaurant, not once but twice!

My memories of my own grandmother are few; she died when I was about eight. My paternal grandmother had died some years earlier in the UK and I have almost no memory of her. The strongest memory I have of her is when she bribed me to go to Sunday school with the offer of making me a new dress. In my memory she was fierce, but I now know that she was nursing her husband, who had Alzheimer's, and that she had very high blood pressure herself (which ultimately killed her).

I have two daughters and neither of them partnered during their twenties or thirties.

The experiences of other friends showed me that being a grandmother seemed hugely enjoyable. I observed with particular delight the development of one friend's three grandchildren, who shared part of my summer holidays over a fifteen-year period. Their growing-up happened so fast. One year we had a baby, a toddler and a preschooler, then, in the blink of an eye, we had bird-watching and boogie boards. Another blink, and we had adolescence, breaking voices and curves.

But nothing was happening on that front in my family. And then my elder daughter met a delightful man. He had been married previously and already had grown-up children. They were undecided about whether to try for their own child, and by the time they agreed to give IVF a go, she was over forty and it just didn't happen. On the sidelines, my heart broke for her and there was little meaningful comfort I could offer. But I know they eventually made peace with the situation and moved on.

A few years passed and then my younger daughter, still without a life partner, announced that she intended to go it alone. Both my elder daughter and I became fully engaged in the whole process, from the earliest talks at Melbourne IVF to the successful birthing of my adorable granddaughter. Elder daughter was the birth partner for her sister—a wonderful decision that set in place a deep connection between the two girls, as well as with the newest girl in the family.

I arrived at the delivery suite half an hour after the birth. My elder daughter was in a bathing costume, having helped her sister shower during contractions. There was a lot of water everywhere, a lot of laughter and, best of all, a beautiful bright-eyed little girl nestled in her mother's arms, a proud aunty along-side. To this day, that love has only deepened and my granddaughter just adores her aunty. I know it might sound like a cliché, but I still believe birth is a miracle.

Mother and baby came to stay with me for the first few weeks. As the new mother learned how to cope with breast-feeding and sleep deprivation, my role was to make lots of food, have lots of baby cuddles, do whatever I could to maximise sleep time for mother. But most of all, I marvelled at the existence of this small, perfect person. I felt such joy and awe as I gazed on her flawless face, the silkiness of her cheeks, the sweep of her eyelashes that trembled with a tear, the tiny fingers and toes, and then there was the clutch of her finger, the sigh of contentment as she settled into her basket.

Somehow the passing of time has changed since my own daughters were babies. With my grandchild, I have been amazed at the speed of her development and wanted to hang on to those early months to better remember them. We are now nearly four years into the life of this precious child and she delights me anew on every occasion. Being with her has been pure pleasure.

•

I miss photograph albums. I own a treasured but very battered album with old sepia and black-and-white photos recording the early days of my parents' courtship, their subsequent travels, my babyhood and that of my siblings, as well as many highlights of our later years. The album ends with lovely images of my own children as babies, all taken well before the digital revolution. I have pored over these photos hundreds of times: just a glimpse of Mum and Dad walking among the cherry blossom in Japan, or of my eldest daughter with her father, stirs rich memories and profound emotions.

Like everyone, I have hundreds of images on my phone and have printed and framed several of them, but scrolling through my digital file of photos doesn't stir the same emotions. It does, however, remind me yet again how fast time has flown in the life of my granddaughter: I had forgotten that day she wore my sunglasses, or when she was on the swing in the park for the first time, or when she helped me mix a birthday cake. Others probably handle their digital files more cleverly, but mine are so jumbled that they frustrate me when I search to locate a specific photo to illustrate a point or a place or a moment in time.

An important part of the pleasure for all of us is the joy with which my elder daughter has embraced being an aunty. There is no trace of resentment or envy, just wholehearted enjoyment of the moment. And she is so good at playing in a really focused way with my granddaughter, who is now right into games of the imagination.

'Say you are driving the fire truck, Aunty L...'

'Say you are the captain of the ship, Grandma...'

This little girl can spend a concentrated hour with a box of Duplo, a brilliant hand-me-down from a dear friend whose own child had outgrown it. It is a large collection of pieces, with trucks and cars of all shapes and sizes, an aeroplane, a police car and fire truck, a house complete with wardrobes and drawers to stuff full of treasures. I love playing with her and listening to her create stories of who is doing what in her Duplo world. But when I dare suggest that the character with the grey hair might be me, she says scathingly, 'No, Grandma, you have white hair…' So far she hasn't shown much interest in dolls, although she does have a small felt mouse that she tucks into its cardboard bed.

•

Being a responsible single mother is a challenge. My daughter has firm ideas about child-rearing, and happily, it seems to me, most are based on common sense. She understands that her child must be able to separate from her without anxiety, so that daycare is enjoyable, not a torment, and so that she can go about earning a living and have a social life. In this she has succeeded admirably. On the occasions that I have collected my granddaughter from daycare, she is always happy to see me, if a bit reluctant to leave whatever game she is engaged in.

My daughter also insists that her daughter explain herself rather than have tantrums. I often hear: 'Use your words to tell me…' Her child is allowed to try and fail if necessary: 'I can do it myself…'—whether she is dipping fingers of toast into a soft-boiled egg in an eggcup, pulling up her underpants or climbing onto a stool to watch me at the kitchen bench. Of course, I sometimes hover with concern. Can she really climb up onto that stool? Can she really serve herself a helping of mashed sweet potato without tipping it all over herself and the table? The answer, of course, is that she can—but hey, what does it matter if a blob of sweet potato ends up on the floor?

Her curiosity is amazing, as is her excitement at seeing something new. 'I saw Mother Earth,' she told me after her first plane ride. Her mother has always enjoyed a new experience and a few facts, and I am delighted that she takes her daughter to places like the Melbourne Museum, Scienceworks, exhibitions at the National Gallery of Victoria, the zoo and so on. Their weekends are crammed with activities.

The only downside is that my daughter's house is on the other side of the city, where most of her close friends live. It is quite an excursion for her to visit me, so I get to see my granddaughter mostly for sleepovers or at family lunches and dinners. Unlike some grandparents, I have never had any desire to be a babysitter and take on one or more days a week to totally devote myself to my grandchild. I am too busy myself for this to happen, but we do all share a holiday once or twice a year; at these times I am entranced with my granddaughter's developing vocabulary and understanding of quite abstract concepts. During our recent holiday in Queensland, she tried to explain gravity to me.

•

With my well-known engagement in all things culinary, I have been especially interested in my granddaughter's food life. I have had to acknowledge (having forgotten that her own mother went through a stage of almost only eating toast with peanut butter, and later had a fixation with lamb cutlets) that young children quickly learn that food is a wonderful power game. Today she may love carrots, but tomorrow will refuse to touch them. She will weep with frustration if I fail to remember that she likes her dinner served in several bowls, so she can help herself: pasta in one bowl, grated cheese in another and the broccoli on a separate plate. Silly of me to forget this, as my own strong preference is to serve dishes to the centre of the table, rather than dole out individual dollops.

She often eats dinner on her own, as bedtime is still quite early for her, but at family lunches we are all at the table together and she is offered the same selection as everyone else. Currently, her favourites are salmon, ocean trout, pasta and savoury homemade meatballs. She enjoys most vegetables and crunchy salad items, although her willingness to try new food seems to change in a random way. Her favourite snacks are crackers and cheese and apple and cheese. For dessert, she likes rhubarb and yoghurt or blueberries and yoghurt. As the child of a modern and informed mother, her intake of sugar and salt is carefully controlled. But that does not prevent a bit of birthday cake or a small serve of ice-cream. Whenever she is at my place, she has her own 'cino', which is really just steamed milk. I love the fact that she is appreciative of food and that her treats are greeted with big smiles.

When I had small children to influence or entertain, we did not have a plethora of screens to contend with. This little person can guide me around a smartphone with ease. 'No, Grandma, you should press *pause*,' or 'It's on the ABC Kids app, Grandma…' She listens to stories on her smartphone after lights out: *Winnie-the-Pooh*, *Paddington*, *Snugglepot and Cuddlepie* and others I haven't heard of. She is allowed to watch *Play School* and *Bluey* fairly regularly.

She shows no interest in the Wiggles, but her all-time favourite, I am a bit worried to admit, is the Disney story *Moana*. Her favourite outfit is a twirly skirt, like Moana's. And she likes to impart bits of Moana's philosophy to me. Moana is a strong female character committed to the cause of saving her community, and my granddaughter goes to great lengths to explain her heroine's battles against the forces trying to sabotage her. I confess that I have had to watch the movie myself to get the context, and I've even googled some of the references, which seem more than far-fetched to me.

But books are still her favourite, which of course delights me and her mother, as we are all book lovers. I think she would be happiest if someone read stories to her for hours on end. I gave her *Milly-Molly-Mandy*, which I remembered fondly; I have to say that I now find the stories too long and very tedious. But she seems to enjoy them. I have also tried *The Complete Adventures of Snugglepot and Cuddlepie*, which did not retain her interest as much as the audiobook version. More successful has been Tim Winton's *Into the Deep,* about a young girl who is frightened of deep water. I am sure I read this story to her with conviction, as I am frightened of deep water myself. My granddaughter is just starting to feel relaxed on a beach, so she listens very closely. At my apartment I keep a bookshelf well stocked with books for her and at home she has many more.

One of the results of being a later-in-life grandmother is that there are lots of things I can't do with her. I cannot run with her in the park or throw and catch balls. I cannot comfortably push her in a stroller up the steep path to my apartment. I can no longer lift her with ease into and out of the bathtub, although I can sit on the stool beside it and help play games with her bath toys. My companionship is pretty well confined to listening to her with full attention, reading stories, joining in games of the imagination, walking to the park to watch her on the swings and—very soon, I hope— helping her learn to cook with pleasure.

I would love to help her make some muffins and scones, grate cheese for gozleme. And I would love her to help me make an apple or a berry tart, or dips with yoghurt and herbs. I could show her how to roll a bit of fresh egg pasta, or dough for a focaccia. If she is interested, we could have many happy times together in the kitchen for years to come.

But I resist considering her future. I know I will probably not be there for her eighteenth birthday, or her other major life milestones. This is too sad to dwell on.

I do speculate as to what sort of future we are developing here in Melbourne, Australia, for a bright and curious young woman who is not wealthy. Will the enormous and disgraceful inequities in our education system still exist, where one school has overwhelmingly grand facilities and another has draughty, inadequate classrooms? Will our cities still be as congested? Will the major transport projects presently under construction cope with the expected population growth? Will the car still be given primacy in all planning? Will people have significantly reduced the waste they produce? Will we still have physical books to read and parks to play in? Will we give more of a helping hand to single parents so they can choose how to manage their time between parenting and other work? Will we help to foster an even more diverse Australia? And will Indigenous Australians have the same opportunities as my granddaughter? Will the health and education authorities have finally agreed to introduce a positive program of pleasurable food education into every school to help all children make good food choices? As I write this in 2019, more than 2000 schools and early-learning centres all round Australia have joined the Stephanie Alexander Kitchen Garden movement. But there are still many thousands of children who have not yet had the chance to understand how life-changing this program can be.

·

My granddaughter understands that she has a donor, not a daddy, and so far seems to take this in her stride. She sometimes casually mentions her 'brothers' to me—there are at least four other half-siblings—'diblings' is the correct term for donor siblings, I've been told—all boys. The donor seems to have a relaxed and interested attitude towards all of these young children. He invites the mothers and children to gatherings once or twice a year, which I found startling when I first heard about it. Now, I just see it as another piece of a brave new world that I can admire, if not fully understand.

My granddaughter has brought me closer to both of my daughters, especially when we share her special moments. My daughters have understood so many of the things that parents have to contend with as we guide and help our cherished children grow and learn. This child looks so much like her mother that she has reminded me of long-ago happy holidays with both of my girls. She has also helped her aunty relax and know that she is loved and valued wholeheartedly. And she has helped me to reflect on the early years of both my daughters: on how quickly one forgets and on how precious those years are.

I have experienced incredible joy and spent many happy hours with my granddaughter. I so want her to live a fulfilling life, have realistic expectations and great friendships, and to remember our time together with love.

Contributors

Stephanie Alexander AO is regarded as one of Australia's great food educators. Her reputation was earned through her thirty years as an owner-chef in several restaurants, as the author of seventeen books and hundreds of articles about food matters, and for her groundbreaking work in creating the Stephanie Alexander Kitchen Garden Foundation. Stephanie believes there is no greater joy than sharing food, conversation and laughter around a table.

Maggie Beer was born in 1945. Maggie is not just an Australian food icon, but an important part of any discussion about food and flavour. Maggie's husband, Colin, daughters, Saskia and Elli, and especially their six grandchildren are vital ingredients in her life, as are music, reading, gardening and spending time with friends.

Judith Brett is Emeritus Professor of Politics at La Trobe University and a political historian who has written extensively on the non-labour side of Australian politics. *The Enigmatic Mr Deakin*, her biography of Alfred Deakin, won the 2018 National Biography Award. Her most recent book is *From Secret Ballot to Democracy Sausage: How Australia Got Compulsory Voting*. She has three daughters and a granddaughter.

Jane Caro AM was born in London in 1957. She is a Walkley Award-winning columnist, author, feminist and novelist. She has two children and two grandchildren. Both her parents are still alive, so she has high hopes of also being a great-grandmother one day.

Elizabeth Chong AM was born in 1931 in Guangzhou, China, and came to Australia when she was three. She is the daughter of William Wing Young, who, with Wing Lee, commercialised the recipe of the dim sim. She is well known for her television appearances on *Good Morning Australia*. As a result of her Chinese Cooking School (1960–2016), she is a loved and admired teacher. She has four children, five grandchildren and two great-grandchildren.

Cresside Collette was born in Colombo, Ceylon (now Sri Lanka), in 1950 and is a tapestry artist. She was a foundation weaver of the Australian Tapestry Workshop. She has taught tapestry weaving and drawing at RMIT University and regularly takes tapestry tours to France and the UK. She has two sons and is the delighted grandmother of a two-year-old granddaughter.

Ali Cobby Eckermann is an award-winning writer of poetry, memoir and fiction. Her poetry collections include *little bit long time*, *Kami* and her most recent, *Inside My Mother*. Her verse novel *Ruby Moonlight* won the 2013 NSW Premier's Literary Award for Poetry and Book of the Year Award. Ali was awarded the inaugural Windham–Campbell Literature Prize from Yale University in 2017.

Helen Elliott was born in Melbourne in 1947. She is a journalist and literary critic. She has two children and four granddaughters. She also has a large garden.

Helen Garner has written novels, stories, screenplays and works of non-fiction. Among her many awards are the Melbourne Prize for Literature, the Windham–Campbell Literature Prize for non-fiction and the Australia Council Award for Lifetime Achievement in Literature. Her books include *Monkey Grip*, *The Spare Room*, *This House of Grief*, *Everywhere I Look*, *Stories*, *True Stories*, *The Children's Bach* and *Yellow Notebook*. She has a daughter and three grandchildren.

Anastasia Gonis is a passionate book lover, writer, reviewer and interviewer. She loves the smell and feel of printed books, and also loves cooking and baking, trees, the sound of the rain and wind, and loyal friends. She has four grandchildren and one on the way.

Glenda Guest won the 2010 Commonwealth Writers' Prize Best First Book for *Siddon Rock*, and her highly acclaimed second novel, *A Week in the Life of Cassandra Aberline*, was published in 2018. After growing up in Western Australia, she has moved way too often, and now lives in Merimbula, NSW, for the third time. Glenda has a daughter and a granddaughter she sees rather less often than she would like.

Katherine Hattam was born in Melbourne in 1950. She has three children and two grandchildren. She is also an artist.

Yvette Holt was born in Brisbane in 1971. She is a multi-award-winning poet, essayist, editor, stand-up comedienne, and femin_artist photographer of erotic desert landscape and queer votive imagery. Mother of one and grandmother of three, Yvette has lived in the Central Australian desert for more than ten years.

Cheryl Kernot is one of Australia's 100 National Living Treasures and was a senator and leader of the Australian Democrats in the 1990s. She was one of Australia's first female cricket umpires and patron of the Australian Women's Cricket Team. Post-politics, she taught at the University of Oxford and then at UNSW's Centre for Social Impact. She has one daughter, two grandchildren and was birth partner for Olivia Mirembe and her three Ugandan sons.

Ramona Koval is a writer and journalist. She is an honorary fellow in the Centre for Advancing Journalism at the University of Melbourne. Her recent books include *Bloodhound: Searching for My Father* and *By the Book: A Reader's Guide to Life*. She is working on a new book about what it means to be human. Mother of two daughters and grandmother of five granddaughters and a grandson, she spends her days writing and cooking diverse meals for picky young eaters.

Alison Lester writes and illustrates books for children. She travels often to remote Indigenous communities, where she helps people turn their stories into books.

Joan London was named a Western Australian State Living Treasure in 2015. Her collected stories are published as *The New Dark Age*. Her first novel, *Gilgamesh*, won the *Age* Book of the Year for Fiction in 2002, and *The Good Parents* won the Christina Stead Prize for Fiction in 2009. Her third novel, *The Golden Age*, won many prizes, including the Prime Minister's Literary Award for Fiction in 2015. She has two children and four grandchildren.

Jenny Macklin was the longest-serving woman in the Australian House of Representatives and the first woman to be elected deputy leader of a major political party. She has delivered many important social reforms, including our first national paid parental leave scheme. She's a feminist, a mother of three and a grandmother of two (so far).

Auntie Daphne Milward was born in Mooroopna, near Shepparton, Victoria. Auntie Daphne is a Yorta Yorta Elder, an artist and a cultural teacher. Throughout her working life, she had many senior roles in private and public life, including her work with a range of Aboriginal advocacy and support organisations. She has two daughters and three grandsons.

Mona Mobarek is a retired schoolteacher of Islamic Studies. She was born in Cairo, Egypt, in 1962 and migrated to Australia in the late sixties. She and her husband, also Egyptian, live in the leafy suburb of Lower Plenty in Melbourne and enjoy travelling. Mona also enjoys sewing and playing music for her family. She has two children and two grandchildren.

Carol Raye was forty-one when she first arrived in Australia from England on the SS *Oriana*, with her husband and their three children. She is ninety-seven and has three grandchildren and a lifetime of memories of a happy marriage and a very rewarding career as a ballerina, theatre and film actress and television producer. She now enjoys watching the changes in the world through the eyes of her grandchildren.

Emeritus Professor Gillian Triggs is the Assistant High Commissioner for International Protection with UNHCR. She was the president of the Australian Human Rights Commission from 2012 to 2017 and president of the Asian Development Bank Administrative Tribunal prior to accepting her position with UNHCR. Now living in Geneva, Gillian is able to spend more time with her grandchildren, who live in Paris.

Célestine Hitiura Vaite is a Tahitian grandmother. She has written three successful novels, has four children, two grandsons and another one on the way. She lives on the South Coast of NSW and loves teaching her grandchildren about nature.